Quick & Delicious Bread Machine Recipes

Quick & Delicious Bread Machine Recipes

Norman A. Garrett

Sterling Publishing Co., Inc. New York

Library of Congress Cataloging-in-Publication Data

Garrett, Norman A.
    Quick & delicious bread machine recipes / by Norman A. Garrett.
        p.   cm.
    Includes index.
    ISBN 0-8069-8812-6
    1. Bread.   2. Automatic bread machines.   I. Title.   II. Title:
Quick and delicious bread machine recipes.
TX769.G374   1993
641.8'15—dc20   92-37674
                                                                         CIP

10   9   8   7   6

Published in 1993 by Sterling Publishing Company, Inc.
387 Park Avenue South, New York, N.Y. 10016
© 1993 by Norman A. Garrett
Distributed in Canada by Sterling Publishing
% Canadian Manda Group, P.O. Box 920, Station U
Toronto, Ontario, Canada M8Z 5P9
Distributed in Great Britain and Europe by Cassell PLC
Villiers House, 41/47 Strand, London WC2N 5JE, England
Distributed in Australia by Capricorn Link Ltd.
P.O. Box 665, Lane Cove, NSW 2066
Manufactured in the United States of America
All rights reserved

Sterling ISBN 0-8069-8812-6

Acknowledgments

This book could not have been written without the assistance of those who encouraged the project, provided some of their favorite recipes for conversion to bread-machine recipes, and then tasted the bread.

In particular, I'd like to thank Carol Lundgren, who offered a great deal of encouragement and who contributed some personal recipes. Margaret Stillions was enthusiastic about the book and was always willing to share her many years of baking experience as well as some excellent recipes. My children, Rachel, Ethan, Joshua, Aaron, and Emily, helped to prepare the recipes, monitored the baking bread, and tested the finished product. Finally, my wife, Margie, provided encouragement, helped to convert recipes, and tasted much of the bread.

CONTENTS

INTRODUCTION

My first bread book, *Great Bread Machine Recipes*, had such a good response that I continued to acquire, convert, test, and prepare bread machine recipes to share with my friends. I tried to develop recipes that would be interesting, somewhat unusual, healthful, and fun to prepare. The result is this book. Because the recipes came from such a variety of countries, I grouped the recipes geographically and, where possible, provided the bread's name in the original language.

The recipes contained in this book were obtained from many sources, including family recipe files, friends and associates, old cookbooks, and even flour sacks. Since bread recipes vary greatly, all must be converted in order to work in bread machines. The result is rarely similar to the original recipe.

Each recipe in this book has been subjected to a rigorous process of conversion and experimentation. Let me explain how I learned to do this and how you, too, can convert your favorite bread recipes for use in your bread machine.

After I overcame my initial fear of experimenting with my machine, I began to record the good recipes and to make notes on the bad ones for future reference. Once I figured out how the machine worked, I wrote some computer software to assist me in developing recipes. The software helped me experiment with fewer failures, and I began to formulate a set of rules for bread machine recipes that, when adhered to, usually yielded good results.

The recipes in this book are the result of this experimentation. As you will see, I have included many different types of recipes using different grains, flours, seeds, and other ingredients. Baking different kinds of breads is an exciting and tantalizing activity, particularly for bread lovers.

Today's heightened health consciousness demands that you know what you're eating. These breads contain only natural ingredients. With a bread machine, you can select recipes that not only appeal to your palate but give you a nutritional boost. Diets need not eliminate bread, as long as you can produce wholesome bread with few empty calories. To help you evaluate the recipes, I've calculated the nutritional values for each of the breads in this book.

There are many bread machines on the market, but not all will bake the same. The machines vary in motor size, baking capacity, cycle types and lengths, baking options, and appearance. Testing these recipes on different machines, I found considerable variation in the quality of the bread they produced. All of the recipes in this book were tested on Hitachi and Welbilt machines. I have tried to adjust the recipes to work in most other available machines, but where modifications might be necessary, they are indicated in the recipes. Be sure to read all the notes for each recipe.

Feel free to experiment. Experimentation allowed me to develop most of the recipes in this book. Once you become familiar with the basic bread ingredients, you'll be able to make substitutions, convert old (standard) bread recipes, and even produce your own creations.

Consider these recipes as a beginning, and make your own notes in the margins of this book. Watch the machine work. Become familiar with its sounds, its cycles, and the texture of the doughs it produces. Familiarity with your machine will lead you to strike out on your own to try new and wonderful tastes in bread. Happy baking!

GETTING TO KNOW YOUR BREAD MAKER

Basic Operation

Although bread machines come in various shapes, sizes, and capacities, they all share common characteristics and principles of operation. They're all designed to make bread making easy, quick, and complete. Other than your placing the proper ingredients in the baking pan, pressing a few buttons, and removing the bread when it's finished (and slicing it, of course), the machine does all the work.

After the ingredients are placed in the pan and you start the machine, the following cycles are completed:

1. Initial mix
2. First rise
3. "Punch down"
4. Second rise
5. Bake
6. Cool-down

The length of each cycle depends upon the make and model of your machine. Some machines skip the second rise, and bake after the first rise. Other machines have alternate settings that let you select a double or single rise (often called the quick bread cycle). Whatever your machine's configuration, you need to become familiar with the way it works so that you can tap its full potential for making delicious loaves of bread.

Capacities

Each machine has a maximum capacity. Capacities are usually either 1 pound or 1½ pounds. Because overloading the machine can cause motor damage or dough overflows, it isn't wise to exceed the rated capacity of your machine.

I've seen ads for machines that can bake 3-pound loaves, but the fine print usually reveals that this will only work for a dense bread that doesn't rise much. In general, I don't recommend baking loaves much larger than your machine can handle because of the strain this places on the motor.

What about baking a loaf smaller than the rated capacity? On most machines, that will work fine. The recipes in this book are presented in both 1-pound and 1½-pound sizes. If you have a 1-pound machine, limit yourself to baking 1-pound loaves. If you have a 1½-pound machine, feel free to try both recipe sizes.

Table 1 shows the capacity differences among bread machines currently on the market. You can determine the capacity of your machine from the owner's manual by checking the white-bread recipe that came with the machine. If the recipe calls for 2 cups of bread flour, you have a 1-pound machine. If it calls for 3 or more cups, you have a 1½-pound (or greater) capacity machine.

Table 1—Bread Machine Capacities

Flour Amount (Basic White Bread (Recipe)	1 Pound	1½ Pound	1½+ Pound
2 cups	X		
2.5	X		
3		X	
3.5			X
3–4			X

Note: Determine the amount of flour called for in the basic white-bread recipe for your machine. This chart will tell you the capacity of your machine based on that amount. If you do not have access to the basic white-bread recipe that came with your machine, assume that it has a 1-pound capacity.

Baking the Dough Yourself

All of these machines let you bake the dough yourself. Simply extract the dough after the first rise is complete. If your machine has a dough setting, it will beep when it is time to remove the dough. You can then punch it down, knead it, and place it in bread pans or on cookie sheets for a final rise and baking.

Adding Ingredients

Some machines have a mix-bread setting, which will beep when it is time to add raisins, seeds, or other ingredients to the dough. Since not all machines have this capability, I have developed the recipes in this book so that all ingredients can be placed in the pan in the beginning. However, if you have a mix cycle, you can use that cycle, particularly in the recipes calling for seeds, nuts, or raisins. The advantage to adding these ingredients in a mix cycle is that they receive less pounding. Raisins, for example, will usually remain whole when the mix-bread setting is used.

Crusts

Baking times vary on bread machines. Most machines offer you the option of selecting the darkness of your crust. The control for this will usually determine the baking temperature of your bread and will not alter the length of the baking cycle. Setting the control for a darker crust will increase the temperature of the oven. On the other hand, I found that turning the dial on the Welbilt machine to the lightest crust setting actually caused some breads to have uncooked dough in the middle. It will probably take a few loaves for you to determine the optimum setting to accommodate both your machine's capabilities and your personal taste. Once you determine that setting, make a note of it, because you will probably want to bake all of your loaves with that same setting.

Knowing Your Own Machine

You will need to get used to your particular machine. When testing the recipes in this book, I found considerable variations between the different machines I used. Become familiar with two parts of the baking process as they apply to your specific machine: the optimum consistency of your dough, and the sound of your machine as it goes through the cycles.

Dough Consistency

Dough consistency and each machine's ability to deal with different dough consistencies are important and vary widely. Some machines work best with a runny dough (more liquid content). Others have powerful motors that can easily handle stiffer doughs. Observe your bread as it mixes. Make a mental note of the dough consistency. Then, when the bread is finished, note the texture of the bread. Learn to compare the finished texture to the consistency of the dough. Soon, you will be able to accurately predict the texture of the bread by looking at the dough immediately after mixing. This skill is important if you want to make any recipe modifications.

Machine Sounds

As you use your machine, also note the typical sounds it makes as it progresses through the various cycles. Once you become familiar with the normal sounds, you will be aware when the motor is making unusual noises, indicating that the motor is being overworked, which can damage the machine.

Service and Cleaning

Cleaning

If you want consistently good bread from your machine, make sure it remains clean. Take two or three minutes after each loaf has baked to clean the machine. This will yield consistently better loaves and will assure that your machine stays in peak operating condition.

The difficulty of cleaning the machines varies according to the design. The Hitachi and similar machines use a bucket with the beater drive mechanism built in. Consequently, the cleaning is simply a matter of removing the bread from the bucket, removing the beater, and cleaning the bucket with warm water. On the Welbilt, the beater drive mechanism is not part of the bucket and must be cleaned after each use. This cleaning is more difficult and sometimes results in crumbs in the bottom of the baking chamber.

I have found that a damp kitchen washcloth will pick up most crumbs from the baking chamber. I have tried mini-vacuums, canned air, and other methods such as turning the whole unit upside down and shaking it, but find the simple washcloth the best (and the least messy).

All bread machines have a special, nonstick surface in the bread pan. Take care with this surface. Do not use any abrasive cleaners or scouring pads on the inside of the bread pan, or you will damage the nonstick surface. Try not to pry stuck breads with knives, forks, or other hard objects that may scratch the pan's surface. If you must pry, use a rubber or soft plastic device of some kind (like a rubber spatula). If you take care of your bread pan, it will give you many future loaves of bread.

The machines, such as the Welbilt and DAK, in which the beater mechanism is part of the housing rather than part of the bread bucket, also have a small plastic washer. Be careful with this washer. Don't lose it. Remember to rinse it off and dry it after each loaf of bread. Without the washer, you won't have a good seal between your bucket and the bottom of your baking chamber, and leakage will occur.

If you have an accident with your bread machine (overflow or other big mess), wait until it cools down and take your time cleaning it. Most baked-on bread can be removed with warm water, and that's the recommended cleanup. I've had my share of disasters, and I have managed to clean all of them up without even using soap. Just warm water and a washcloth have always been all that was needed.

Lost and Damaged Parts

There are generally no user-serviceable components in the bread machine, other than those just mentioned. However, there are parts that are easily lost or damaged, which you can replace yourself. Most prominent on the list is the mixer beater. Since it is a small, removable part, it is easily misplaced. Make sure that you replace the beater in the bucket after each cleaning. That will minimize the potential for losing it.

The plastic washer that fits beneath the bread bucket will wear out over time. If your machine has one of these, it might be a good idea to order a replacement to have on hand, since this washer is an inexpensive item.

Bread Pan

The other major removable component is the bread pan itself. Be careful of the nonstick surface. If you damage the surface to the point where bread sticks to it, you'll have to replace the bread pan. As long as you're able to remove the bread from the pan, don't be concerned about small scratches.

Major Repairs

If any other problems arise with your machine, you will probably have to send it out for repair. The control panel, for example, will sometimes cease to function and will need to be replaced. You should obtain an estimate before authorizing any major repairs on your machine, because it's possible that the cost of repairs will exceed the cost of the machine. The likelihood is that your machine will have a long, productive life, and that it will give you many hours of trouble-free bread baking if you'll simply keep it clean and ready for the next loaf.

Troubleshooting Guide

There are many variables that can affect your bread. Those listed below are all problems I have experienced while making bread in my own machines. You may encounter some not listed here. Before you write off the bread machine completely or send it out for repairs, think the problem through and make sure that you have accounted for all the possible reasons for the problem. These reasons could include wrong crust settings, improper baking cycles, measuring ingredients improperly, using stale ingredients, failure to check for power outages during baking (which will recycle your machine), and, finally, curious children pushing buttons.

Stuck Dough Beater

If your dough beater is difficult to remove after baking a loaf of bread, try using some shortening on the shaft before installing the beater and placing dry ingredients in the pan first. In the machines where the beater is self-contained in the pan, soak the beater in water for a few minutes after removing the bread. In the DAK/Welbilt-type machines, the beater will stay with the loaf of bread and is rarely a problem to remove.

Leakage of Liquid

This might be a problem on the DAK/Welbilt machines or others whose pans have a hole in the bottom to accommodate the dough beater. These machines should have dry ingredients placed in the bread pan first. Liquids should be added last. Also, check to make sure that you have the rubber sealing washer in the proper position before locking the pan in place. Then make sure that the pan is securely locked before adding ingredients.

Recipe Flop

Make sure that you've added the proper quantities. It's easy to become distracted while setting up a recipe and to miscount your ingredients. Also, check that you chose the correct setting when baking the bread. Finally, be sure that your ingredients are fresh and that you're using the proper ingredients.

Loaf-Size Variation

The size of your loaf will vary according to the ingredients. While the weight of two loaves of bread may be the same, their size and appearance may vary greatly. This is due to the different ingredients used. In general, breads using gluten-rich bread flour will rise more than breads using flours with less gluten content. Rye breads, for example, will be small and will have a dense texture with a dark crust. The loaf sizes of the recipes in this book refer to weight, not to finished size.

Spoiled Ingredients

You must be cautious with fresh eggs and fresh milk. Do not use either of these ingredients in a delay-bake cycle (available on some machines), where you set the timer to start the bread at a later time. Milk is all right if the delay is not more than an hour or two, but I would not recommend that eggs be used in any recipe that will not be started immediately. If you want to use a recipe calling for eggs on a delay bake, consider using powdered eggs instead of fresh eggs. If you want to use milk in a delayed recipe, use dry milk and add the proper amount of water to compensate.

Collapsing Dough

Your dough probably rose too long. Since the timer cycles are not programmable on most machines, you may consider reducing the yeast by $1/2$ teaspoon to get less rising. Check to make sure that the machine was not recycled during the process. Recycling can occur after brief power outages. It may also occur when children (or curious adults) press machine buttons. If a power outage occurs and you're aware of it, you can remove the dough from the machine and finish the process by hand, baking the bread in the oven.

Strong Yeast Flavor

It's possible that too much yeast was added. Reduce the amount of yeast by ½ teaspoon and try again.

Failure to Rise

This can be a complex problem with many possible causes. Any of the following will inhibit rising:

- Using flour with low-gluten content (pure rye flour, wheat flour, etc.)
- Too much salt in the recipe. Salt is a yeast inhibitor.
- Too little sugar in the recipe. Sugar feeds yeast and promotes rising.
- Old yeast. Yeast expires. Check your yeast supply and make sure you're using fresh yeast. Old yeast will not activate and rise properly.
- Dead yeast. This may be caused by adding hot ingredients. For example, if your recipe calls for some ingredients to be boiled before being added to the mix, don't add them until they've have time to cool. Adding ingredients that are too hot will kill your yeast.

Uneven Top

This usually indicates too little liquid in the recipe. However, on some breads, such as rye breads, where less rising takes place, this may be a normal occurrence.

Collapsed Top

This is usually caused by too much liquid in the recipe. Cut the liquid back by 2 tablespoons and try again. Be careful not to make your bread dough too stiff, because some machines have underpowered motors that will not be able to handle stiffer dough, particularly in the 1½-pound recipes. Also, be aware that some recipes use ingredients that are going to add liquid to the dough during the baking cycle, and a collapsed top might be normal. I found this to be the case with breads using fresh cheeses.

Rancid Taste

Check your whole-grain ingredients. Whole-grain flours, wheat germ, and similar ingredients should be kept in the refrigerator or freezer. They spoil rapidly when left at room temperature. White flours are not subject to the same type of spoilage and can be left in the cupboard for storage.

White Spots

This is flour that has stuck to the side of the pan during the mixing process and has not mixed into the dough. When the bread rises and bakes, this flour sticks to the outside of the loaf. While not a taste problem, it can present a cosmetic problem. The solution is to look into the baking pan after the mixing has taken place. If there is flour stuck to the sides of the pan, take a rubber spatula, remove it from the sides, and mix it in with the dough.

Soggy Crust

You left the bread in the pan too long after the baking cycle was completed. Some machines have cooling cycles that will cool the bread and remove the moisture. Soggy crust is not as great a problem on these machines, but it is still a good idea to remove the bread and place it on a cooling rack as soon as the final beep is heard.

Improper Mix

This happened to me when I forgot to replace the dough beater after cleanup from the previous loaf. Now I watch the initial mix for a minute or so when I first turn on the machine. I can see the mixing taking place. If the motor is running, but no mixing is happening, check the dough beater. If it has been left out, stop the machine, replace the beater, and start the cycle over.

Inconsistent Size & Texture

If you bake the same recipe and get different results, blame the weather. Weather is actually a large factor in baking, as temperature and humidity influence the amount of rising that takes place.

Lost Dough Beater

If you have the type of machine whose beater stays in the loaf when the bread is removed from the baking pan, check the last loaf of bread. I had a loaf of bread ready to give to a friend for testing, only to realize that I was about to give away the dough beater, too! Get in the habit of cleaning your pan right away and putting everything back in the machine. Then your beater will always be where you want it: in the pan ready to bake.

CONVERTING EXISTING RECIPES

Naturally, after you've had time to experiment with your bread machine, you'll want to try great-grandma's recipe. However, you will notice that her recipe was not designed to work in a bread machine. But, fortunately, most yeast-bread recipes can be converted to work in bread machines.

The key is to make sure the recipe is yeast-based. Although yeast is reliable and easy to use, this was not always the case. Recipes that are more than 40 or 50 years old will usually use a chemical, rather than an organic, leavening. Chemical leavenings include baking soda and baking powder, and these leavenings do not have the same properties as yeast. Don't attempt to convert recipes that are not yeast-based for use in your bread machine.

Converting a recipe to work in your machine is not difficult, but it is computationally intensive work. Have a calculator handy if you want to attempt a conversion. You'll also want a sheet or two of paper to write down the totals and the new, converted recipe.

This chapter will take you through the steps for converting a "regular" recipe to one you can try in your machine. It may take one or two trials to perfect the recipe, but the changes are good that you can successfully make the conversion. Before converting a recipe, make sure that it is a yeast-bread recipe. As mentioned above, bread machines are not designed to handle batter breads or breads using chemically based leavenings.

Four Basic Steps

1. Cut the recipe down so that it will make one loaf. Many recipes are designed to make two loaves. You will need to cut such recipes in half, because you'll need a single-loaf recipe.
2. Determine the parameters of your particular bread machine.
3. Determine the liquidity ratio of the recipe. This ratio represents the "stiffness" of the dough, an important factor, because your machine has a rather narrow range of doughs it can handle.
4. Determine the overall bulk of the recipe. You don't want a recipe that's too large for your machine.

Let's look at each of these steps in turn, with particular attention to the details involved in each step. Once you've accomplished a few conversions, you won't need to refer to this book, because the steps are not really as complex as they might seem at first.

Reducing Recipe Size

Most recipes will tell you how many loaves they make. Some will even tell you the approximate size of each loaf. Cut the recipe so that it will make one loaf and write down the new recipe.

If the recipe doesn't say how many loaves it makes, you can make a rough judgment by looking at the amount of flour required. A 1-pound loaf of bread will require about 2 cups of flour. Thus, if your recipe calls for 6 cups of all-purpose flour, you can probably figure that it will make three 1-pound loaves or two 1½-pound loaves.

Determining Machine Parameters

Since each machine varies in its capacity and motor power, you must determine the acceptable ranges for your machine in two categories: liquidity ratio and bulk. Table 2 shows the acceptable liquidity-ratio ranges. To find your machine's

Table 2—Bread-Machine Liquidity Ratios

Ounces Liquid ⅛ c = 1 oz	Cups of Flour			
	2	2½	3	3½
5	2.9–3.5	3.6–4.4	4.3–5.3	5.0–6.2
6	2.4–3.0	3.0–3.6	3.6–4.4	4.2–5.2
7	2.1–2.5	2.6–3.2	3.1–3.7	3.6–4.4
8	1.8–2.2	2.3–2.8	2.7–3.3	3.2–3.9
9	1.6–2.0	2.0–2.4	2.4–3.0	2.8–3.4
10	1.4–1.8	1.8–2.2	2.2–2.6	2.5–3.1
11	1.4–1.7	1.6–2.0	2.0–2.4	2.3–2.8

Notes: 1. Shaded boxes show the most common bread-machine ratio ranges. 2. Ratio is computed by dividing dry ingredients by liquid. 3. Higher ratios indicate stiffer dough; lower ratios indicate more liquid dough.

range, look at the basic white-bread recipe that came with the machine. Determine the number of cups of flour called for. Follow that column until you find the row that shows the number of ounces of liquid (water or milk) called for in the recipe. In that box you will find the ratio range for your machine. Highlight or write down the ratio range. (On page 124, you can note this and other information about your bread machine.)

Bulk is determined by the number of cups of flour called for in the basic white-bread recipe for your machine. If the recipe calls for 2–2½ cups of flour, you have a 1-pound machine. If the recipe calls for 3–4 cups of flour, you have a 1½-pound (or greater) machine.

Once you known the parameters of your machine, you can skip this step and move right from Step One to Step Three.

Determining Liquidity Ratio

Now, you must determine the liquidity ratio (dough stiffness) of the recipe you're trying to convert. Table 3 on page 24 is a handy chart that you can duplicate and use each time you convert a recipe. To use the chart, simply fill in the ingredients and the amount called for in the original recipe. Write the amounts in decimals (so that you can use your calculator to add them later) in the appropriate column. For example, if the recipe calls for 2½ cups of flour, enter 2.5 in the DRY Cup column. You'll have to determine whether the ingredient is dry or wet. In general, use the form that the ingredient is in when you add it. An exception to this would be an ingredient that's going to melt when heat is applied. Typical ingredients in this category would include butter, margarine, fresh cheese, and shortening.

Some ingredients shouldn't be computed. Don't include the following ingredients in the calculation:

1. Yeast
2. Raisins or nuts added at the mix cycle
3. Seeds added at the mix cycle

You should count raisins, nuts, and seeds added initially as dry ingredients. The general rule is that if the ingredient will add to the stiffness of the dough, count it as a dry ingredient.

After you've entered all the ingredients, total each column and place the sum in the subtotal box. Then multiply each subtotal by the multiplier specified and place the result in the total box. Add the totals for dry ingredients together for a grand total and do the same for wet ingredients Finally, divide the dry grand total by the wet grand total to compute the ratio for this recipe.

For best results, the ratio should fall within the liquidity-ratio-range designation for your machine (see Step Two). If this ratio only misses by a few points, it will probably be satisfactory. If the ratio for the recipe is below the range, your dough might be too wet. Try a slight reduction in liquid ingredients or an increase in dry ingredients and recalculate. If the ratio is above the range, it's too dry. Either reduce the dry ingredients slightly or add liquid.

Chances are that you'll still need to experiment to get the recipe just right, but this calculation will give you a good start and place you well beyond the "trial and error" stage.

Table 3—Dough Liquidity Calculation Worksheet

Ingredient	DRY			WET			
	tsp	tbs	cup	tsp	tbs	cup	oz
Subtotal							
Multiplier		3	48		3	48	6
TOTAL							
GRAND TOTAL							
Liquidity Ratio							

Instructions: 1. Use decimals for fractions (.5 teaspoon, etc.). 2. Use a calculator to subtotal each column. 3. Multiply the subtotal by the multiplier to obtain the total. 4. Add the dry totals and wet totals separately to obtain the grand total. 5. Divide the dry grand total by the wet grand total to get the liquidity ratio.

Determining Bulk

You certainly don't want to overflow your machine with your test recipe, so make sure that the bulk doesn't exceed the capacity of your machine. If you have a 1-pound machine, your recipe should not call for more than 2½ cups of flour. A 1½-pound machine is limited to about 3½ cups of flour. If you need to fine-tune the recipe, be sure you make equal adjustments to both the wet and dry ingredients to maintain the liquidity ratio of the recipe.

Improving and Tailoring Your Recipes

After your initial attempt at your newly converted recipe, you may want to adjust it to increase or decrease the bulk, to reduce or increase rise, or to alter the texture or taste. Experiment with the recipe until you've perfected it. Part of the enjoyment of a bread machine is being able to try new and exciting recipes and to be creative. Although the conversion process, as presented here, may seem somewhat better suited to a mathematician than to an artist, science and art go hand in hand in bread baking. Once you get to know your machine and your ingredients, you'll feel comfortable making substitutions or even trying brand-new creations from scratch.

RECIPE POINTERS

Recipe Sizes

Two sizes are given for each of the recipes in this book. Smaller sizes are possible, but I don't recommend them. In experimenting, I found that the machines tended to overbake ¾-pound loaves and that such loaves typically were too dry. Consequently, I decided to include only the two sizes that can be accommodated by virtually all bread machines.

Recipe sizes refer to finished weight, not dimensions. The finished dimensions of the bread will depend to a great extent upon baking conditions, amounts of yeast used, and types of ingredients. A 1-pound loaf of white bread, for example, might be larger than a 1½-pound loaf of rye bread; rye tends to be more densely textured than white.

Modifications for Specific Machines

I've tried to include recipes that will work in any machine. With the 1-pound recipes, I found virtually no difference when testing the recipes in different machines. With the 1½-pound loaves, however, I noted that some machines will not tolerate a stiff dough as well as others do. For those recipes, I have noted that you might consider adding 1 or 2 tablespoons more liquid in certain machines. This addition will lower the liquidity ratio slightly, making the dough less stiff. Some motors appear to labor under the load of 1½ pounds of stiff dough. If your machine seems to be having trouble kneading dough, add a little liquid to the recipe. As mentioned previously, you'll come to recognize the normal sounds of your machine, and you'll be able to identify those situations when slight recipe modifications are needed.

The other major difference between machines is in their rise cycles and in the amount of yeast called for. I've tried to optimize the amount of yeast in the recipes to be suitable to all machines. When more yeast is needed for a certain machine, the notes for the recipe will indicate it. Be sure to read the notes for each recipe before trying it. There may be modifications for your particular machine.

A few machines, such as the Hitachi, have quick bread cycles that allow you to bake a loaf quickly (single rise, rather than the usual double rise). When using this cycle on your machine, double the amount of yeast that's normally called for or consult your owner's manual for the proper yeast adjustment.

Ingredients

There's a wide variety of ingredients called for in these recipes. Many are available at your local supermarket, but some must be purchased at health-food stores. The following is a summary of important information about some of the main ingredients used in the recipes in this book.

White Flours

There are two main types of white flours: all-purpose flour and bread flour. Both varieties are available in most grocery stores. Bread flour is higher in gluten content than all-purpose flour, and bread flour will rise more. Most of the recipes in this book call for bread flour; however, there are a few that specifically call for all-purpose flour. Substituting all-purpose flour for bread flour is permissible, but such a substitution will slightly change the texture of the bread and cause it to rise less.

Whole Grains

Whole-wheat flour This flour is ground from the complete wheat berry and contains the wheat germ and the wheat bran. It is coarser and heavier than white flour, and it does not rise as much as white flour. I purchase fresh wheat in bulk and grind it myself for the best-tasting bread, but this is beyond the capability of most people. Grocery stores carry whole-wheat flour, usually right alongside the white flour.

Bran Bran is the outer covering of the kernel of wheat or oat. It is rich in fibre and is called for in small quantities in some recipes. Recently, much has been said about the benefits of oat bran. Both oat and wheat bran are available at most grocery stores.

Wheat germ This part of the wheat grain is readily available in grocery stores. Like bran, it is used sparingly in recipes. Wheat germ should be kept in the refrigerator after the container is opened.

Rye flour Rye flour is very low in gluten content, and it will not rise when used by itself. You'll note that most of the recipes in this book call for a mixture of rye and another flour with a higher gluten content that will let the bread rise.

Barley flour Barley flour lends a sweet taste and smooth texture to bread. Most recipes call for it in combination with white or wheat flour. You will probably have to go to a health-food store to find barley flour.

Cracked wheat As its name implies, this is part of the wheat berry. It is very hard and usually requires some soaking before use. Cracked wheat is widely available at health-food stores and can often also be found in grocery stores.

Seven-grain cereal This cereal has an appearance similar to cracked wheat. It consists of seven grains, including wheat, barley, corn, and oats. It is available at health-food stores.

Oats Use rolled oats (oatmeal) for your oat recipes. Just use the type available at the grocery store. When measuring rolled oats, pack them down into the

1 egg = 1/4 cup

measuring cup to get a full measure.

Quinoa This flour is imported from South America. It was a staple grain of the Incas in ancient times. Quinoa has one of the highest protein contents of any grain. It gives bread a somewhat nutty flavor.

Buckwheat This strong-tasting flour has attracted a loyal band of aficionados. Buckwheat is usually used in small quantities, but if you like its strong flavor, you can use it in combination with whole-wheat flour.

Liquids

Water is called for in most recipes. It should be used warm (between 100 °F and 110 °F). I've found that hot tap water works fine. Don't heat the water any hotter, since water that's too hot can kill the yeast.

Milk When milk is called for in a recipe, I use 1 percent fat or skim milk. In fact, the nutritional counts in the recipes in this book are calculated using values for 1 percent fat milk. If you don't have fresh milk on hand, try using dry milk and adding the requisite amount of water to the recipe. Milk should usually be warmed to 100–110 °F. The microwave heats milk well at 45 seconds on HIGH. Be careful not to add overheated milk to the mix, or you'll kill the yeast.

Buttermilk You can use buttermilk in its fresh form, or you can purchase buttermilk powder and mix it as needed. I do the latter. I don't particularly like to drink buttermilk, and recipes usually only call for small amounts. In most recipes, it's safe to substitute low-fat or skim milk for buttermilk. You may sacrifice some flavor, but your bread will have a lower fat content.

Cream There are several types of cream available at most grocery stores: heavy cream, light cream, whipping cream, and half-and-half. Some recipes call for heavy or light cream, but I've found that whipping cream works fine in most cases where cream is called for. Note that *whipping cream* and *whipped cream* are different. Whipped cream has had sugar added and is already in whipped form. Whipping cream comes in a carton and pours like milk.

Eggs Most of the recipes in this book have been formulated to call for whole eggs rather than portions of eggs or egg whites. However, if you're concerned about the cholesterol in eggs, you may use any commercially available egg substitute. Use 1/4 cup (4 tablespoons) of egg substitute to replace each whole egg. If you use powdered eggs, use 1/4 cup of mixed powdered eggs instead of one whole egg.

Butter Many of the recipes in this book call for butter. You may substitute margarine or vegetable oil in the same quantities. Butter, however, will provide the most flavor. I keep my butter in the freezer, because spoilage is a big problem with real butter. When I need butter, I remove it from the freezer, cut off the required quantity, and return the stick to the freezer. It only takes a few minutes for the cut portion to reach room temperature. There is no need to melt the butter or margarine before adding it to the recipe, but it is best if the butter chunks are 1 tablespoon or less in size.

Olive oil I've used olive oil exclusively in these recipes. I think olive oil tastes best. Additionally, olive oil has no cholesterol. However, if you prefer another type of cooking oil, such as canola, corn oil, or any other vegetable oil, you may substitute freely. If you use olive oil, use a good grade of extra-virgin olive oil.

Other Ingredients

Salt Salt, a yeast inhibitor, is necessary in most recipes. If you are on a salt-restricted diet, you can eliminate the salt from the recipes. You should know, however, that if you do so, the characteristics of the bread will change. It will rise differently, and it may rise too much and then collapse. The resulting texture may also be different. Keep in mind that other ingredients often have a salt content. If you are on a salt-restricted diet, check the nutritional values for each recipe to see if there are "hidden salts" in the recipe. Butter, for example, is one of the ingredients that has a sodium content. Avoid using salt substitutes as alternatives. They are chemically based and they don't have the yeast-inhibiting properties of real salt. Not only will they do no good, but they may cause other chemical reactions that will change the properties of your bread.

Yeast The recipes in this book call for yeast in teaspoons. I use Red Star active dry yeast, and I buy it in bulk. If kept in the refrigerator, it will last a long time. In fact, with my bread machine running, a supply of yeast doesn't last long at all. If you use cake yeast, you will need to make the conversion from teaspoons. If you purchase yeast in packets at the grocery store, one packet contains one scant tablespoon, or about 2¼ teaspoons of yeast. Do not use rapid-rise yeast in these recipes.

Because there are differences in cycle lengths and the yeast-dispensing mechanisms available on a few machines, not all bread machines use the same amount of yeast in the large recipes. If a recipe does not rise enough, try adding an extra ½ teaspoon of yeast.

Yeast feeds on sugars and is inhibited by salts. It likes a warm environment, but too much heat will kill it. Most traditional bread recipes will require you to "proof" your yeast before using it. Proofing involves mixing the yeast with sugar and warm (105–110 °F) water to allow it to become active before adding it to the recipe. Proofing is not necessary with bread machines, but it is a good technique to use if you want to make sure your yeast is active (not too old). Yeast can be placed directly into the bread pan. When it touches liquid, it will begin activating.

Sugars and sweeteners These are necessary in all bread recipes because they provide food for the yeast. Recipes in this book call for sugar (white, granulated, or brown), honey, syrup, or molasses. Molasses comes in various types, but I use blackstrap when baking. I have tried others, and I haven't noticed any appreciable difference in the outcome, so use whichever molasses you happen to have on hand if a recipe calls for it. If the recipe calls for olive oil and honey or molasses, measure the olive oil first and don't rinse off the spoon. The honey or molasses will slide right off the greased spoon into your pan!

Gluten Gluten is necessary for rising to occur. White flours contain plenty of gluten, but some whole-grain flours don't. I've found that some gluten flour added to the mix when using a low-gluten flour will make for better rising and texture. Gluten flour can be purchased at any good health-food store. A few recipes call for gluten flour, but most make it optional. Some people are allergic to gluten. Those individuals should stick to low-gluten flours, including rye and quinoa.

Dough enhancer This product is difficult to find. Even health-food stores may not carry it. You may find it at baking specialty stores. Dough enhancer is a powder produced from tofu (soybean) that makes the dough smoother. Commercial bakers often use dough enhancer to obtain the smooth-textured bread you buy at the store. If you want to try it, it's listed as an optional ingredient in some of the recipes.

Spices, nuts, and seeds These ingredients are called for in a wide variety of recipes. I have found most of the spices, seeds, and nuts called for in these recipes at the grocery store. If you can't find them, you might try your health-food store, which will usually stock some of the lesser-known spices. Feel free to experiment with spices, adding more of the spices you like and deleting those you don't. Often it's the blend of spices that makes the flavor, rather than any single spice, especially in those recipes calling for two or three different spices.

You'll find that as you bake more breads, your spice cabinet enlarges. Eventually, you'll have a stock of almost any spice called for in a recipe. Preserving spices and seeds is not a problem, but preserving fresh nuts is. A few recipes call for fresh chopped nuts. Use any type of nuts you enjoy, but keep in mind that nuts will go rancid if not used in a short period. Keep your supply of fresh nuts rotated.

Sourdough starter In the section on American pioneer breads, there's a recipe for sourdough starter on page 44. You can use this recipe, locate another (any good bread-recipe book will have one), or simply get starter from your local bakery or from a friend. Once you have starter going, you can keep it replenished and never run short. Starter is used in sourdough recipes and can be added as you would any other ingredient.

Order of Ingredients

There are two ways to place ingredients in the baking pan: dry ingredients first or wet ingredients first. Most machines call for dry ingredients first, so that order is used in this book. Actually, dry first will work in all machines, unless you want to use a timed-bake function. In that case, you won't want to activate the yeast until the baking process starts, so wet ingredients will have to go first and yeast last. The machines that recommend dry ingredients first call for yeast as the first ingredient, followed by the other dry ingredients and, finally, the liquids. That is the order followed in these recipes. If your machine calls for wet ingredients first or if you are trying to use a timed-bake feature, add the ingredients to the pan in reverse order from that order listed (start at the bottom of the list and work your way to the top).

Preparation of Ingredients

Most bread recipes call for all ingredients to be at room temperature, except for liquids, which are sometimes called for at 105–110 °F. I've experimented with this and have not had real problems adding refrigerated ingredients. Rather than worry too much about it, just try setting all of your ingredients out first and then add them. Once you get to the refrigerated ingredients, they've usually approached room temperature anyway.

When warm water is called for, it should be in the 105–110 °F range. I used to use a thermometer to make sure that the water was the correct temperature; however, I gave up on that when I found that hot tap water usually falls within that temperature range. Because hot tap water varies, make sure that yours is not too hot. Too hot presents a much bigger problem than too cold.

Milk can either be measured and then left to reach room temperature, or you can use your microwave to warm it up. Just be sure that if you use the microwave, you don't overheat the milk, which is easy to do. If you do overheat it, let it sit until it cools down to below 110 °F before adding it to the bread pan.

For measuring flour and dry ingredients, I use the dip-and-level method. Just dip your measuring cup into the flour and level it with a knife or other flat edge.

Substitutions and Modifications

I recommend that you try the recipes as-is, the first time. Then, if you want to make substitutions or modifications, experiment all you want. I have found that the best way to experiment is to alter one item at a time. If you alter too many things at once and the recipe fails, you won't be able to determine the cause of the failure. However, if you only changed one ingredient, you will know that the alteration was the only variable that could have caused the failure.

You can freely make the substitutions mentioned in the ingredients section, including margarine for butter, low-fat or skim milk for buttermilk, egg substitutes for whole eggs, and all-purpose flour for bread flour. Keep in mind, however, that these substitutions will alter the original recipe somewhat and results will be different.

Avoid the use of chemically based substitutes such as sugar and salt substitutes. These chemically based products may taste the same in coffee or soft drinks, but they break down differently from real sodium or sugar in baking and they won't work properly with yeast breads. It is better to simply eliminate salt, for example, than to use a salt substitute. Yeast feeds fine on sugar, but it doesn't have much of a taste for aspartame.

Once you've gained a feel for a recipe and for your machine, feel free to experiment. Most of the recipes in this book were developed that way, and you can have a lot of fun trying new and wonderful ideas. It is best to begin with established recipes and make successive alterations until you arrive at the perfect bread. Be sure to keep a log of your changes and the results. That way, you can learn as you go and won't repeat mistakes. It also helps to have a basic understanding of the principles of baking with yeast and of the characteristics of the ingredients you are using.

Slicing Bread

When you get that loaf out of the machine, it smells wonderful. In fact, it has probably permeated the whole house with the unmistakable odor of baking bread! You may want to dig in and eat the whole loaf right on the spot. Of course, you can do that. There is nothing better than fresh hot bread. However, if your aim is to slice the bread and keep it for a few days or to use it for tomorrow's breakfast or lunch, then you'll need to slice it carefully.

Bread is best sliced after it's had a chance to cool completely. It then regains some of its stiffness and it's much easier to handle. Slicing hot bread is a bit like trying to slice jello. As you cut, the bread gives, and it's difficult to get a good straight slice.

For best results, remove your bread from the machine as soon as the all-done alarm sounds. Place the bread on a cooling rack and let it cool completely (probably an hour or so). While many machines now include cooling cycles, they can't completely cool the bread because the loaf is still in the pan where moisture and heat are trapped.

To slice the bread, use a serrated knife designed especially for slicing bread. Use a sawing motion and let the knife do the work. Putting too much downward pressure on the bread will smash it down and give you uneven slices.

I inherited a meat slicer, and I don't use it for meat at all. I *have* found it to be a wonderful bread slicer. Just set the thickness and the serrated blade cuts right through the cool loaf. If you have a slicer, and the loaf is too big for it (Welbilt loaves are too big for my slicer), cut the loaf in half lengthwise, making two half-circles. Then, slice each half-loaf with your slicer.

Nutritional Values

I am convinced that much of the consumer motivation behind the boom in bread machine sales is due to a desire to eat healthful foods. Whole-grain breads are wonderful sources of nutrients, have no chemical preservatives, and taste great.

Each recipe is followed by nutritional values. I've purposely left the nutritional values at the loaf level, rather than trying to determine the value of a single slice. Everyone will slice bread differently. If you want to know the nutritional values for a slice of your bread, estimate what percentage of the total loaf the slice is and multiple that number by the nutritional values shown for the size you baked. For example, if a 1½-pound loaf is cut into 10 slices, multiple the nutritional value by 0.1 to obtain the values for one slice.

The nutritional values are estimates only, and they should not be construed as anything else. They were derived by using the *Encyclopedia of Food Values*, by Corinne T. Netzer (Dell, 1992). Each of the ingredients in the recipes was calculated and totalled for each size of loaf. Here is an explanation of the values used:

Calories are total calories for the loaf.

Protein is measured in grams. Breads are not high in protein, but when taken with other foods (for example, meats, or legumes such as beans), a healthful combination is made.

Carbohydrates are also measured in grams. Carbohydrates, especially from whole-grain sources, provide a good ratio of nutrients to calories (the opposite of "empty calories") and should constitute 45–48 percent of your daily intake of calories.

Fat is listed as total fat and saturated fat. You should try to reduce the amount of fats in your diet. Saturated fats should be avoided as much as possible. Government recommendations are that you limit your total calories from fat to 30 percent of your daily intake of calories. Saturated-fat calories should be limited to only 10 percent. In addition to giving you the amount of total fat and saturated fat in grams, I have computed the percentage of calories from fat for each recipe. You will note that these breads are very healthful from the standpoint of percentage of calories from fats.

Cholesterol content is measured in milligrams. Cholesterol is only found in animal fats and certain vegetable fats (especially palm oil and coconut oil). Most nutritionists recommend that your total dietary cholesterol intake not exceed 300 milligrams per day.

Sodium, measured in milligrams, can be found in the salt added to the recipe and in the sodium content of some other recipe ingredients. If you are on a low-sodium diet, you can reduce the salt content of the loaf, but remember the limitations discussed previously.

Fibre is a concern to health-conscious people. The fibre content of each recipe is measured in grams. Because fibre takes several forms, the figure given is a total figure that includes both dietary and crude fibre. Most nutritionists recommend at least 25 grams of fibre per day in your diet.

Recipe Notes

Some recipes contain notes regarding variations to be used with certain machines. These notes refer to *classes* of machines. If the note mentions DAK/Welbilt, it refers to those particular machines or any other machine calling for 1¼ cups of liquid, 3 cups of flour, and 1 package of yeast in its basic, 1½-pound white-bread recipe. References to Panasonic/National include any machine calling for 1¼ cups of liquid, 3 cups of flour, and 3 teaspoons of yeast in its basic 1½-pound white-bread recipe. These variations usually only apply to the 1½-pound recipes, although occasionally I have made an alteration for a 1-pound recipe.

Your strategy for testing recipes should be to try the 1-pound loaf first, even if you have a 1½-pound capacity machine. This plan offers three advantages:

1. You can make sure you like the taste and texture of the bread by using a lesser quantity of ingredients for the first test.

2. You can make sure the bread works well in your machine with fewer ingredients at risk.

3. You can make sure that your particular baking conditions won't produce an oversize loaf, with little risk of a mess if they do.

Once you've tested a bread, make alterations to suit your taste, baking conditions, and machine. For example, you can increase or reduce yeast amounts, change the liquidity, try substitute seeds or nuts, or make other ingredient substitutions. I would highly recommend, however, that you try the recipe once before making you own modifications so that you'll have a basis upon which to make your changes and a point of reference. Then, be creative.

Disclaimer

The nutrient values shown with the recipes in this book are approximations only and are shown strictly for comparison. Because nutrient values will vary according to the product brand, quantity, and type of ingredient used, individuals needing specific nutrient values should compute the values themselves. Neither the author nor the publisher represents these values to reflect the exact nutritional content of these recipes.

Results of these recipes will vary according to climatic conditions, proper use of ingredients, make and model of machine used, and freshness of ingredients. All recipes in this book have been thoroughly tested but not on all available machines. The author and publisher make no guarantee as to the results of an individual recipe baked on a particular machine in a specific situation, since the possible combinations of variables are almost endless.

AMERICAN PIONEER BREADS

The recipes in this section are based on old American favorites from various parts of the United States. Because these recipes predate the commercial development of yeast for baking, most of these breads probably started out as baking-powder breads, baking-soda breads, or sourdough breads. In fact, the recipe for *Forty-Niner Sourdough Bread* has changed little since the days of the California gold rush.

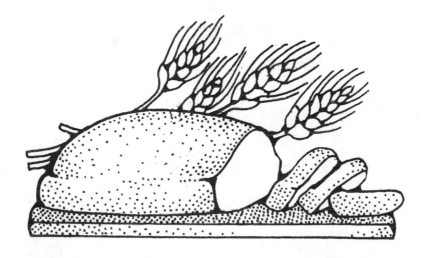

Adobe Bread

Originally designed for the adobe ovens of the American Southwest, this bread tastes just as good when baked in your machine.

1½-pound

1½ teaspoons active dry yeast

3 cups all-purpose flour

1 teaspoon salt

3 tablespoons olive oil

1 cup warm water

1-pound

1 teaspoon active dry yeast

2 cups all-purpose flour

½ teaspoon salt

2 tablespoons olive oil

5 ounces warm water

Notes:

1. For Panasonic/National machines, use 3 teaspoons of yeast for the 1½-pound loaf.
2. For DAK/Welbilt machines, add 2 extra tablespoons of warm water to the 1½-pound loaf.

NUTRITIONAL ANALYSIS			
	1½-POUND	1-POUND	
TOTAL CALORIES	1853	1235	
TOTAL PROTEIN	51	34	GRAMS
TOTAL CARBOHYDRATES	300	200	GRAMS
TOTAL FAT	48	32	GRAMS
TOTAL SATURATED FAT	6	4	GRAMS
TOTAL CHOLESTEROL	0	0	MILLIGRAMS
TOTAL SODIUM	2140	1071	MILLIGRAMS
TOTAL FIBRE	7	4	GRAMS
% CALORIES FROM FAT	23	23	

Adobe Bread II

This is a variation of the adobe-bread recipe. The main difference is the addition of sugar and the deletion of olive oil.

1½-pound

1½ teaspoons active dry yeast

3 cups all-purpose flour

2 teaspoons salt

2 teaspoons sugar

9 ounces warm water

1-pound

1 teaspoon active dry yeast

2 cups all-purpose flour

1 teaspoon salt

1½ teaspoons sugar

6 ounces warm water

Notes:

1. For Panasonic/National machines, use 3 teaspoons of yeast for the 1½-pound loaf.
2. For DAK/Welbilt machines, use 2 extra tablespoons of warm water for the 1½-pound loaf.

NUTRITIONAL ANALYSIS			
	1½-POUND	1-POUND	
TOTAL CALORIES	1526	1020	
TOTAL PROTEIN	51	34	GRAMS
TOTAL CARBOHYDRATES	307	206	GRAMS
TOTAL FAT	7	5	GRAMS
TOTAL SATURATED FAT	1	1	GRAMS
TOTAL CHOLESTEROL	0	0	MILLIGRAMS
TOTAL SODIUM	4272	2137	MILLIGRAMS
TOTAL FIBRE	7	4	GRAMS
% CALORIES FROM FAT	4	4	

Amish Bread

Here is a simple, tasty, white bread with a sweet taste and a wonderfully fluffy texture.

1½-pound

1½ teaspoons active dry yeast

3¼ cups bread flour

1 teaspoon salt

3 tablespoons sugar

4 tablespoons olive oil

9 ounces warm water

1-pound

1 teaspoon active dry yeast

2 cups + 2 tablespoons bread flour

½ teaspoon salt

2 tablespoons sugar

2½ tablespoons olive oil

6 ounces warm water

Note:

For Panasonic/National machines, use 3 teaspoons of yeast for the 1½-pound loaf.

NUTRITIONAL ANALYSIS			
	1½-POUND	1-POUND	
TOTAL CALORIES	2233	1471	
TOTAL PROTEIN	55	37	GRAMS
TOTAL CARBOHYDRATES	360	240	GRAMS
TOTAL FAT	62	39	GRAMS
TOTAL SATURATED FAT	8	5	GRAMS
TOTAL CHOLESTEROL	0	0	MILLIGRAMS
TOTAL SODIUM	2140	1072	MILLIGRAMS
TOTAL FIBRE	7	5	GRAMS
% CALORIES FROM FAT	25	24	

Anadama Bread

The addition of cornmeal gives this rich white bread a somewhat crunchy texture.

1½-pound	1-pound
1½ teaspoons active dry yeast	1 teaspoon active dry yeast
½ cup cornmeal	⅓ cup cornmeal
1 teaspoon salt	½ teaspoon salt
2¾ cups bread flour	1¾ cups + 2 tablespoons bread flour
3 tablespoons molasses	2 tablespoons molasses
1 cup warm water	6 ounces warm water
2½ tablespoons butter	2 tablespoons butter

Notes:
1. For Panasonic/National machines, use 3 teaspoons of yeast for the 1½-pound loaf.
2. For DAK/Welbilt machines, add 2 tablespoons of warm water for the 1½-pound loaf.

NUTRITIONAL ANALYSIS			
	1½-POUND	1-POUND	
TOTAL CALORIES	2023	1403	
TOTAL PROTEIN	52	35	GRAMS
TOTAL CARBOHYDRATES	364	247	GRAMS
TOTAL FAT	37	29	GRAMS
TOTAL SATURATED FAT	19	15	GRAMS
TOTAL CHOLESTEROL	78	62	MILLIGRAMS
TOTAL SODIUM	2208	1117	MILLIGRAMS
TOTAL FIBRE	13	9	GRAMS
% CALORIES FROM FAT	17	18	

Cottage-Cheese Bread

Pioneers used what they had on hand to make bread. This recipe uses ingredients found in the typical pioneer kitchen. Because the loaf will really rise, try the 1-pound recipe first to make sure your machine can handle the size.

1½-pound

1½ teaspoons active dry yeast

¼ cup whole-wheat flour

2¾ cups bread flour

1½ teaspoons salt

½ teaspoon sugar

1 tablespoon sour cream

½ cup cottage cheese

1 egg

2 tablespoons butter

2 tablespoons honey

2 ounces warm milk

1-pound

1 teaspoon active dry yeast

¼ cup whole-wheat flour

1¾ cups bread flour

1 teaspoon salt

½ teaspoon sugar

½ tablespoon sour cream

6 tablespoons cottage cheese

1 egg

1 tablespoon butter

1½ tablespoons honey

1½ ounces warm milk

Note:

For Panasonic/National machines, use 3 teaspoons of yeast for the 1½-pound loaf.

NUTRITIONAL ANALYSIS			
	1½-POUND	1-POUND	
TOTAL CALORIES	1996	1357	
TOTAL PROTEIN	73	52	GRAMS
TOTAL CARBOHYDRATES	330	229	GRAMS
TOTAL FAT	40	25	GRAMS
TOTAL SATURATED FAT	20	11	GRAMS
TOTAL CHOLESTEROL	298	260	MILLIGRAMS
TOTAL SODIUM	3811	2610	MILLIGRAMS
TOTAL FIBRE	10	8	GRAMS
% CALORIES FROM FAT	18	16	

Country Bread

The specifics of the Midwestern origins of this bread are unknown, but it is a wonderfully rich white loaf sweetened by dates and nuts.

1½-pound

1½ teaspoons active dry yeast

2 teaspoons dried lemon peel

3 tablespoons sugar

3 cups bread flour

1½ teaspoons salt

2 eggs

5 tablespoons butter

7 ounces warm milk

3 tablespoons chopped nuts

3 tablespoons chopped dates

1-pound

1 teaspoon active dry yeast

1½ teaspoons dried lemon peel

1½ tablespoons sugar

2 cups bread flour

1 teaspoon salt

1 egg

3 tablespoons butter

5 ounces warm milk

2 tablespoons chopped nuts

2 tablespoons chopped dates

Notes:

1. For Panasonic/National machines, use 3 teaspoons of yeast for the 1½-pound loaf.
2. Dates and nuts may be added during the mix cycle or add them at the beep (if your machine is equipped with one).

NUTRITIONAL ANALYSIS			
	1½-POUND	1-POUND	
TOTAL CALORIES	2609	1662	
TOTAL PROTEIN	75	48	GRAMS
TOTAL CARBOHYDRATES	375	245	GRAMS
TOTAL FAT	90	55	GRAMS
TOTAL SATURATED FAT	42	25	GRAMS
TOTAL CHOLESTEROL	590	312	MILLIGRAMS
TOTAL SODIUM	3448	2282	MILLIGRAMS
TOTAL FIBRE	9	6	GRAMS
% CALORIES FROM FAT	31	30	

Sourdough Breads

Before you begin this you must know how to make the sourdough starter.

Sourdough Starter

This recipe will give you enough starter to begin with. Each time you remove starter to make batter, don't forget to replenish the starter with your leftover batter. Starter is best stored in the refrigerator in a glass container. It improves with age; the older the starter, the more pungent the taste and aroma. Starter age is measured in years, not days, so don't become impatient with it. As your starter matures, it will get better and better.

- Warm a quart jar or similar container by filling it with hot tap water and letting it sit for a few minutes.
- In a pan or microwave oven, heat 1 cup of skim or low-fat milk to 100–110 °F. Remove the milk from the heat and add 3 tablespoons of plain yogurt to the milk.
- Drain the warm water from the jar and wipe it dry.
- Pour the milk-yogurt mixture into the jar and cover it. Note that it is preferable to use a plastic lid, but if your jar has a metal lid, place plastic wrap or waxed paper under the lid before screwing it tight.
- Place the mixture in a warm place and allow it to proof for 24 hours.
- Stir 1 cup of all-purpose flour into the milk-yogurt mixture. Cover, and leave in a warm place for 3–5 days.
- At the end of 5 days, your starter should be bubbly and about the consistency of pancake batter. When it has reached this point, place the jar in the refrigerator for storage.

Making Sourdough Starter Batter

Although sourdough was widely used as a leavening in the last century, it didn't become famous until the gold-rush days of 1848 and 1849. Even with a bread machine, sourdough recipes require a little more patience than other bread recipes because the sourdough batter must be prepared in advance. Here is the procedure for making sourdough batter for any recipe requiring it.

- Remove your sourdough starter from the refrigerator and allow it to reach room temperature (about 6 hours).
- Place 1½ cups of starter in a 2-quart mixing bowl.
- Return the remaining starter to the refrigerator.
- Add 1½ cups of all-purpose flour and 1 cup of warm skim milk and mix well. The batter should have the consistency of a light pancake batter.

- Cover the bowl lightly and let the batter proof for 8–12 hours in an 85–90 °F environment.
- After proofing, use what batter you need for your bread (it can remain out for 1–3 days), but make sure you save at least 1½ cups of batter to replenish your starter.
- Return the remaining batter to your starter pot. Stir and refrigerate.

Many people place the starter directly into the ingredients. While this method will certainly work, it isn't the best way to keep your starter active, because after you remove the starter, you have to add flour and milk and again proof the starter.

I have found it better to use the batter method described above. It tends to keep my starter more active and gives me plenty of batter to use in my recipes. If you use the batter method, place batter in the recipe any time sourdough starter is called for.

Forty-Niner Sourdough Bread

This recipe reflects the way bread was made 150 years ago in the mining camps of California. There is no yeast in this recipe; the sourdough starter is the only leavening present. It yields an authentic, densely-textured, sourdough bread.

1½-pound	1-pound
1½ teaspoons sugar	1 teaspoon sugar
1½ teaspoons salt	1 teaspoon salt
3 cups bread flour	2 cups bread flour
½ cup sourdough starter batter	¼ cup sourdough starter
¾ cup warm water	½ cup warm water

Notes:

Instructions for baking: Stop your machine after the dough has been thoroughly mixed. Set the machine to a timed bake. Give the sourdough at least 6–8 hours to rise before the bake cycle begins. If you do not have a timed cycle on your machine, let the dough sit for 6–8 hours, and allow the bread to undergo a complete mix/bake cycle.

I find it handy to mix this bread in the evening and set it to finish baking about breakfast time.

For DAK/Welbilt machines, for the 1½-pound loaf add an extra 2 tablespoons of warm water.

NUTRITIONAL ANALYSIS			
	1½-POUND	1-POUND	
TOTAL CALORIES	1756	1129	
TOTAL PROTEIN	57	37	GRAMS
TOTAL CARBOHYDRATES	354	228	GRAMS
TOTAL FAT	8	5	GRAMS
TOTAL SATURATED FAT	1	1	GRAM
TOTAL CHOLESTEROL	0	0	MILLIGRAMS
TOTAL SODIUM	3205	2137	MILLIGRAMS
TOTAL FIBRE	7	5	GRAMS
% CALORIES FROM FAT	4	4	

Grumbera Bread

This bread was originally made with real mashed potatoes. For the sake of simplicity, I developed a recipe using mashed-potato flakes. It retains the excellent flavor and light-yellowish color of the original.

1½-pound

1½ teaspoons active dry yeast

½ cup mashed-potato flakes or buds

3 cups + 2 tablespoons bread flour

1½ teaspoons salt

2 tablespoons sugar

5 ounces warm water

2 eggs

4 ounces warm milk

1 tablespoon butter

1-pound

1 teaspoon active dry yeast

¼ cup mashed-potato flakes or buds

2 cups + 2 tablespoons bread flour

1 teaspoon salt

1½ tablespoons sugar

3 ounces warm water

1 egg

3 ounces warm milk

½ tablespoon butter

Note:

For Panasonic/National machines, use 3 teaspoons of yeast for the 1½-pound loaf.

NUTRITIONAL ANALYSIS			
	1½-POUND	1-POUND	
TOTAL CALORIES	2080	1356	
TOTAL PROTEIN	72	47	GRAMS
TOTAL CARBOHYDRATES	360	243	GRAMS
TOTAL FAT	36	20	GRAMS
TOTAL SATURATED FAT	12	6	GRAMS
TOTAL CHOLESTEROL	462	232	MILLIGRAMS
TOTAL SODIUM	3755	2427	MILLIGRAMS
TOTAL FIBRE	7	5	GRAMS
% CALORIES FROM FAT	16	13	

Herb Bread

Excellent with soup or salad, herb bread is also good as morning toast.

1½-pound

1½ teaspoons active dry yeast

1 tablespoon dill weed

3 tablespoons dried parsley

3 tablespoons dried chives

3 cups bread flour

1 teaspoon salt

1½ tablespoons sugar

7 ounces warm water

1½ tablespoons butter

2 ounces warm milk

1-pound

1 teaspoon active dry yeast

2 teaspoons dill weed

2 tablespoons dried parsley

2 tablespoons dried chives

2 cups bread flour

½ teaspoon salt

1 tablespoon sugar

5 ounces warm water

1 tablespoon butter

1 ounce warm milk

Note:

For Panasonic/National machines, use 3 teaspoons of yeast for the 1½-pound loaf.

NUTRITIONAL ANALYSIS			
	1½-POUND	1-POUND	
TOTAL CALORIES	1803	1198	
TOTAL PROTEIN	57	38	GRAMS
TOTAL CARBOHYDRATES	333	221	GRAMS
TOTAL FAT	25	16	GRAMS
TOTAL SATURATED FAT	12	8	GRAMS
TOTAL CHOLESTEROL	49	32	MILLIGRAMS
TOTAL SODIUM	2214	1116	MILLIGRAMS
TOTAL FIBRE	9	6	GRAMS
% CALORIES FROM FAT	12	12	

Indian Bread

Cornmeal and cream give this bread a distinctive flavor and texture.

1½-pound

1½ teaspoons active dry yeast

2¼ cups + 2 tablespoons all-
purpose flour

¾ cup cornmeal

1½ teaspoons salt

2 eggs

3 tablespoons butter

4 ounces cream

3 ounces warm water

2½ tablespoons honey

1-pound

1 teaspoon active dry yeast

1½ cups + 2 tablespoons all-
purpose flour

½ cup cornmeal

1 teaspoon salt

1 egg

2 tablespoons butter

2½ ounces cream

2 ounces warm water

2 tablespoons honey

Note:

For Panasonic/National machines, use 3 teaspoons of yeast for the 1½-pound loaf.

NUTRITIONAL ANALYSIS			
	1½-POUND	1-POUND	
TOTAL CALORIES	2316	1520	
TOTAL PROTEIN	64	39	GRAMS
TOTAL CARBOHYDRATES	343	233	GRAMS
TOTAL FAT	76	49	GRAMS
TOTAL SATURATED FAT	41	26	GRAMS
TOTAL CHOLESTEROL	570	307	MILLIGRAMS
TOTAL SODIUM	3417	2261	MILLIGRAMS
TOTAL FIBRE	12	10	GRAMS
% CALORIES FROM FAT	30	29	

Onion Bread

This is a tasty, high-rising loaf with country origins. Although the recipe has been modified to use dried ingredients for easier bread machine baking, the original flavor is still evident.

1½-pound

1½ teaspoons active dry yeast

3 cups bread flour

1½ tablespoons grated Parmesan cheese

½ teaspoon salt

2½ teaspoons sugar

2 tablespoons dried onion-soup mix

1 tablespoon butter

9 ounces warm water

1-pound

1 teaspoon active dry yeast

2 cups bread flour

1 tablespoon grated Parmesan cheese

¼ teaspoon salt

1½ teaspoons sugar

1½ tablespoons dried onion-soup mix

½ tablespoon butter

6 ounces warm water

Note:

For Panasonic/National machines, use 3 teaspoons of yeast for the 1½-pound loaf.

NUTRITIONAL ANALYSIS			
	1½-POUND	1-POUND	
TOTAL CALORIES	1744	1153	
TOTAL PROTEIN	56	38	GRAMS
TOTAL CARBOHYDRATES	327	220	GRAMS
TOTAL FAT	21	12	GRAMS
TOTAL SATURATED FAT	10	5	GRAMS
TOTAL CHOLESTEROL	37	20	MILLIGRAMS
TOTAL SODIUM	3110	2054	MILLIGRAMS
TOTAL FIBRE	7	4	GRAMS
% CALORIES FROM FAT	11	10	

Plymouth Bread

An old New England favorite, this bread combines basic ingredients to produce a firm, tasty loaf.

1½-pound

1½ teaspoons active dry yeast

2¾ cups bread flour

1½ teaspoons salt

4 tablespoons cornmeal

4 tablespoons molasses

1½ tablespoons butter

7 ounces warm water

1-pound

1 teaspoon active dry yeast

2 cups bread flour

1 teaspoon salt

2½ tablespoons cornmeal

2½ tablespoons molasses

1 tablespoon butter

5 ounces warm water

Note:

For Panasonic/National machines, use 3 teaspoons of yeast for the 1½-pound loaf.

NUTRITIONAL ANALYSIS			
	1½-POUND	1-POUND	
TOTAL CALORIES	1872	1316	
TOTAL PROTEIN	49	35	GRAMS
TOTAL CARBOHYDRATES	354	249	GRAMS
TOTAL FAT	25	17	GRAMS
TOTAL SATURATED FAT	12	8	GRAMS
TOTAL CHOLESTEROL	47	31	MILLIGRAMS
TOTAL SODIUM	3278	2183	MILLIGRAMS
TOTAL FIBRE	9	6	GRAMS
% CALORIES FROM FAT	12	11	

Southern Bread

This fluffy white-bread recipe has been a favorite in the southern United States. It's excellent sandwich bread.

1½-pound

1½ teaspoons active dry yeast

2 tablespoons wheat germ

1 tablespoon sugar

3 tablespoons dry milk

3 cups bread flour

1 teaspoon salt

1 tablespoon butter

9 ounces warm water

1-pound

1 teaspoon active dry yeast

5 teaspoons wheat germ

½ tablespoon sugar

2 tablespoons dry milk

2 cups bread flour

½ teaspoon salt

½ tablespoon butter

6 ounces warm water

Notes:
1. For Panasonic/National machines, use 3 teaspoons of yeast for the 1½-pound loaf.
2. For DAK/Welbilt machines, use 2 additional tablespoons of warm water for the 1½-pound loaf.

NUTRITIONAL ANALYSIS			
	1½-POUND	1-POUND	
TOTAL CALORIES	1755	1154	
TOTAL PROTEIN	61	42	GRAMS
TOTAL CARBOHYDRATES	329	218	GRAMS
TOTAL FAT	20	12	GRAMS
TOTAL SATURATED FAT	8	4	GRAMS
TOTAL CHOLESTEROL	34	18	MILLIGRAMS
TOTAL SODIUM	2236	1135	MILLIGRAMS
TOTAL FIBRE	8	6	GRAMS
% CALORIES FROM FAT	10	9	

Sunflower-Seed Whole-Wheat Bread

The seeds and shredded coconut in this bread give it a nutty flavor. The whole-wheat flour gives it a hearty taste and texture. It's a great breakfast bread.

1½-pound

1½ teaspoons active dry yeast

¾ cup bread flour

2 tablespoons sunflower seeds

2 tablespoons shredded coconut

½ teaspoon salt

2¼ cups whole-wheat flour

1 tablespoon olive oil

1 cup warm water

4 tablespoons honey

1-pound

1 teaspoon active dry yeast

½ cup bread flour

1½ tablespoons sunflower seeds

1½ tablespoons shredded coconut

¼ teaspoon salt

1½ cups whole-wheat flour

½ tablespoon olive oil

5½ ounces warm water

1½ tablespoons honey

Notes:

1. For Panasonic/National machines, use 3 teaspoons of yeast for the 1½-pound loaf.
2. For DAK/Welbilt machines, use 2 additional tablespoons of warm water for the 1½-pound loaf.

NUTRITIONAL ANALYSIS			
	1½-POUND	1-POUND	
TOTAL CALORIES	1794	1177	
TOTAL PROTEIN	54	36	GRAMS
TOTAL CARBOHYDRATES	344	227	GRAMS
TOTAL FAT	31	20	GRAMS
TOTAL SATURATED FAT	6	4	GRAMS
TOTAL CHOLESTEROL	0	0	MILLIGRAMS
TOTAL SODIUM	1096	555	MILLIGRAMS
TOTAL FIBRE	37	24	GRAMS
% CALORIES FROM FAT	16	15	

War Bread

Legend has it that this bread was first baked during the American Revolution. Oats and cornmeal were added to make the flour go further, creating a great loaf of healthful bread.

1½-pound

1½ teaspoons active dry yeast

2½ cups all-purpose flour

1 teaspoon salt

¼ cup whole-wheat flour

¼ cup cornmeal

¼ cup rolled oats

10 ounces warm water

1½ tablespoons molasses

½ tablespoon butter

1-pound

1 teaspoon active dry yeast

1¾ cups all-purpose flour

1 teaspoon salt

2½ tablespoons whole-wheat flour

2½ tablespoons cornmeal

2½ tablespoons rolled oats

7 ounces warm water

1 tablespoon molasses

½ tablespoon butter

Notes:

1. For Panasonic/National machines, use 3 teaspoons of yeast for the 1½-pound loaf.
2. For DAK/Welbilt machines, use 2 additional tablespoons of warm water for the 1½-pound loaf.

NUTRITIONAL ANALYSIS			
	1½-POUND	1-POUND	
TOTAL CALORIES	1678	1165	
TOTAL PROTEIN	52	36	GRAMS
TOTAL CARBOHYDRATES	330	226	GRAMS
TOTAL FAT	15	12	GRAMS
TOTAL SATURATED FAT	5	4	GRAMS
TOTAL CHOLESTEROL	16	16	MILLIGRAMS
TOTAL SODIUM	2174	2160	MILLIGRAMS
TOTAL FIBRE	15	10	GRAMS
% CALORIES FROM FAT	8	9	

MEDITERRANEAN BREADS

The area that surrounds the Mediterranean encompasses a wide variety of cultures. Each country produces different types of bread. In this section, you'll find breads from Greece, Italy, and Portugal.

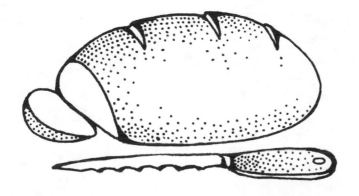

Christopsomo (Greek Christmas Bread)

The slight cherry aroma makes this sweet-tasting bread perfect for parties or special occasions.

1½-pound

1½ teaspoons active dry yeast

3 chopped candied cherries

1 tablespoon chopped walnuts

3¼ cups all-purpose flour

1 teaspoon crushed anise seed

½ teaspoon salt

½ cup sugar

2 eggs

3 ounces warm water

5 tablespoons butter

½ cup warm milk

1-pound

1 teaspoon active dry yeast

2 chopped candied cherries

2 teaspoons chopped walnuts

2¼ cups all-purpose flour

½ teaspoon crushed anise seed

½ teaspoon salt

5 tablespoons sugar

1 egg

2 ounces warm water

3½ tablespoons butter

3 ounces warm milk

Note:

For Panasonic/National machines, use 3 teaspoons of yeast for the 1½-pound loaf.

NUTRITIONAL ANALYSIS			
	1½-POUND	1-POUND	
TOTAL CALORIES	2736	1839	
TOTAL PROTEIN	73	47	GRAMS
TOTAL CARBOHYDRATES	428	289	GRAMS
TOTAL FAT	81	54	GRAMS
TOTAL SATURATED FAT	41	28	GRAMS
TOTAL CHOLESTEROL	586	325	MILLIGRAMS
TOTAL SODIUM	1268	1184	MILLIGRAMS
TOTAL FIBRE	7	5	GRAMS
% CALORIES FROM FAT	26	26	

Italian Whole-Wheat Bread

If you like whole-grain breads, this wheat bread will please your palate. It has a light, wheat flavor and somewhat crumbly texture. If you prefer a smoother texture, add the optional dough enhancer.

1½-pound

1½ teaspoons active dry yeast

1½ tablespoons dough enhancer (optional)

2 cups all-purpose flour

1 cup whole-wheat flour

2 tablespoons wheat germ

1½ teaspoons salt

1½ teaspoons brown sugar

1 tablespoon butter

9 ounces warm water

1-pound

1 teaspoon active dry yeast

1 tablespoon dough enhancer (optional)

1¼ cups all-purpose flour

¾ cup whole-wheat flour

1½ tablespoons wheat germ

1 teaspoon salt

1 teaspoon brown sugar

½ tablespoon butter

6 ounces warm water

Notes:

1. For Panasonic/National machines, use 3 teaspoons of yeast for the 1½-pound loaf.
2. For DAK/Welbilt machines, use 2 additional tablespoons of warm water for the 1½-pound loaf.

NUTRITIONAL ANALYSIS			
	1½-POUND	1-POUND	
TOTAL CALORIES	1585	1037	
TOTAL PROTEIN	55	37	GRAMS
TOTAL CARBOHYDRATES	302	201	GRAMS
TOTAL FAT	20	12	GRAMS
TOTAL SATURATED FAT	8	4	GRAMS
TOTAL CHOLESTEROL	31	16	MILLIGRAMS
TOTAL SODIUM	3209	2139	MILLIGRAMS
TOTAL FIBRE	21	15	GRAMS
% CALORIES FROM FAT	11	10	

Pane Italiano

This simple bread is a staple in Italy. It is easy to make and yields the kind of loaf you associate with traditional Italian bread. It is an excellent base for garlic bread.

1½-pound

1½ teaspoons active dry yeast

3 cups + 2 tablespoons bread flour

1½ teaspoons salt

9 ounces warm water

1-pound

1 teaspoon active dry yeast

2 cups + 2 tablespoons bread flour

1 teaspoon salt

6 ounces warm water

Notes:

1. For Panasonic/National machines, use 3 teaspoons of yeast for the 1½-pound loaf.
2. For DAK/Welbilt machines, use 1 additional tablespoon of warm water for the 1½-pound loaf.

NUTRITIONAL ANALYSIS			
	1½-POUND	1-POUND	
TOTAL CALORIES	1560	1061	
TOTAL PROTEIN	53	36	GRAMS
TOTAL CARBOHYDRATES	312	213	GRAMS
TOTAL FAT	7	5	GRAMS
TOTAL SATURATED FAT	1	1	GRAM
TOTAL CHOLESTEROL	0	0	MILLIGRAMS
TOTAL SODIUM	3206	2138	MILLIGRAMS
TOTAL FIBRE	7	5	GRAMS
% CALORIES FROM FAT	4	4	

Panettone

Because it has a sweet, nutty flavor, this Italian bread is particularly enjoyable as a breakfast toast served with butter and jam.

1½-pound

1½ teaspoons active dry yeast

½ teaspoon dried orange peel

1½ teaspoons dried lemon peel

½ teaspoon salt

3 cups + 3 tablespoons all-purpose flour

6 tablespoons sugar

2 eggs

7½ tablespoons butter

6 ounces warm milk

6 tablespoons raisins

4 tablespoons shredded almonds

1-pound

1 teaspoon active dry yeast

½ teaspoon dried orange peel

1 teaspoon dried lemon peal

½ teaspoon salt

2 cups + 2 tablespoons all-purpose flour

4 tablespoons sugar

1 egg

5 tablespoons butter

½ cup warm milk

4 tablespoons raisins

3 tablespoons shredded almonds

Notes:

1. For Panasonic/National machines, use 3 teaspoons of yeast for the 1½-pound loaf.
2. If your machine has a mix cycle, you may add the almonds and raisins at the beep.

NUTRITIONAL ANALYSIS			
	1½-POUND	1-POUND	
TOTAL CALORIES	3196	2060	
TOTAL PROTEIN	79	49	GRAMS
TOTAL CARBOHYDRATES	448	287	GRAMS
TOTAL FAT	124	82	GRAMS
TOTAL SATURATED FAT	60	40	GRAMS
TOTAL CHOLESTEROL	666	373	MILLIGRAMS
TOTAL SODIUM	1310	1208	MILLIGRAMS
TOTAL FIBRE	11	7	GRAMS
% CALORIES FROM FAT	35	36	

Portuguese Corn Bread

Here is a good, dense, corn bread with a crunchy texture and rich flavor. It is very good with soup or with butter and jelly or jam.

1½-pound

1½ teaspoons active dry yeast

2 cups bread flour

1½ teaspoons salt

1½ cups cornmeal

1 tablespoon sugar

1 tablespoon olive oil

9 ounces warm water

1-pound

1 teaspoon active dry yeast

1¼ cups bread flour

1 teaspoon salt

1 cup cornmeal

2 teaspoons sugar

2 teaspoons olive oil

6 ounces warm water

Notes:
1. For Panasonic/National machines, use 3 teaspoons of yeast for the 1½-pound loaf.
2. For DAK/Welbilt machines, use 2 additional tablespoons of warm water for the 1½-pound loaf.

NUTRITIONAL ANALYSIS			
	1½-POUND	1-POUND	
TOTAL CALORIES	1829	1178	
TOTAL PROTEIN	49	31	GRAMS
TOTAL CARBOHYDRATES	353	227	GRAMS
TOTAL FAT	25	16	GRAMS
TOTAL SATURATED FAT	3	2	GRAMS
TOTAL CHOLESTEROL	0	0	MILLIGRAMS
TOTAL SODIUM	3268	2179	MILLIGRAMS
TOTAL FIBRE	25	16	GRAMS
% CALORIES FROM FAT	12	13	

Portuguese Sweet Bread

Light and sweet, this rich white bread is great at breakfast, spread with jam or jelly.

1½-pound

1½ teaspoons active dry yeast

3¼ cups bread flour

1 teaspoon salt

¼ cup sugar

4 tablespoons butter

2 eggs

5 ounces warm milk

3 ounces warm water

3 tablespoons currants

1-pound

1 teaspoon active dry yeast

2 cups + 3 tablespoons bread flour

½ teaspoon salt

5½ tablespoons sugar

3 tablespoons butter

1 egg

3 ounces warm milk

2 ounces warm water

2 tablespoons currants

Note:

For Panasonic/National machines, use 3 teaspoons of yeast for the 1½-pound loaf.

NUTRITIONAL ANALYSIS			
	1½-POUND	1-POUND	
TOTAL CALORIES	2682	1810	
TOTAL PROTEIN	74	47	GRAMS
TOTAL CARBOHYDRATES	450	303	GRAMS
TOTAL FAT	65	45	GRAMS
TOTAL SATURATED FAT	34	24	GRAMS
TOTAL CHOLESTEROL	556	310	MILLIGRAMS
TOTAL SODIUM	2351	1186	MILLIGRAMS
TOTAL FIBRE	9	6	GRAMS
% CALORIES FROM FAT	22	23	

AFRICAN AND CAUCASIAN BREADS

These few recipes offer a glimpse into the cuisines of these exotic regions. You've probably never tried these recipes before, so here's your chance to please and surprise friends and family with new and exciting tastes.

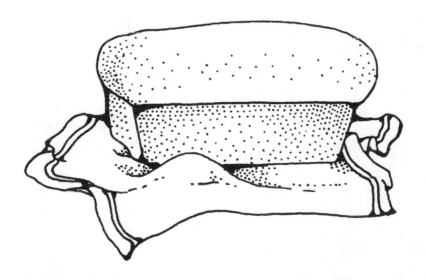

Armenian Pita

Pita cannot be baked in the bread machine, but you can use the dough cycle to mix it and to let it rise. After the first rise, remove the dough and follow the instructions below to bake the small pita loaves. I like to stuff this pocket bread with chicken, tomato, and lettuce.

1½-pound	1-pound
1½ teaspoons active dry yeast	1 teaspoon active dry yeast
1 tablespoon sugar	2½ teaspoons sugar
3 cups all-purpose flour	2 cups all-purpose flour
1 teaspoon salt	½ teaspoon salt
1 tablespoon olive oil	½ tablespoon olive oil
1 cup warm water	5½ ounces warm water

Notes:

1. For Panasonic/National machines, use 3 teaspoons of yeast for the 1½-pound loaf.
2. For DAK/Welbilt machines, use 2 additional tablespoons of warm water for the 1½-pound loaf.

Instructions for baking:

Remove the dough from the machine at the end of the dough cycle (after the first rise). Form the dough into individual balls approximately 2–3 inches in diameter. Place the balls on a greased cookie sheet. Flatten the balls with the palm of your hand until each is about ¾ inch thick. Cut the top of each with a razor blade. Cover them lightly and let the pitas rise for about 20–30 minutes or until about double in volume.

Bake in a preheated, 425 °F oven until brown and crusty (about 20 minutes). Cut the pita loaves in half and split the insides.

NUTRITIONAL ANALYSIS			
	1½-POUND	1-POUND	
TOTAL CALORIES	1661	1095	
TOTAL PROTEIN	51	34	GRAMS
TOTAL CARBOHYDRATES	311	210	GRAMS
TOTAL FAT	21	11	GRAMS
TOTAL SATURATED FAT	3	2	GRAMS
TOTAL CHOLESTEROL	0	0	MILLIGRAMS
TOTAL SODIUM	2140	1071	MILLIGRAMS
TOTAL FIBRE	7	4	GRAMS
% CALORIES FROM FAT	11	9	

Churek Bread

The sesame seeds in this Armenian recipe produce a basic white bread with a distinctive flavor. Traditionally, Churek is baked as a flat, crisp bread. This recipe gives you the flavor of Churek and allows you to bake it in your bread machine. As a variation, you can bake it by hand in a large, flat loaf.

1½-pound

1½ teaspoons active dry yeast

4 tablespoons sesame seeds

1 tablespoon sugar

3 cups all-purpose flour

2 teaspoons salt

1 cup warm water

4 tablespoons butter

1-pound

1 teaspoon active dry yeast

2½ tablespoons sesame seeds

½ tablespoon sugar

2 cups all-purpose flour

1½ teaspoons salt

5 ounces warm water

2½ tablespoons butter

Notes:

1. For Panasonic/National machines, use 3 teaspoons of yeast for the 1½-pound loaf.
2. For DAK/Welbilt machines, use 2 additional tablespoons of warm water for the 1½-pound loaf.

NUTRITIONAL ANALYSIS			
	1½-POUND	1-POUND	
TOTAL CALORIES	2150	1400	
TOTAL PROTEIN	58	38	GRAMS
TOTAL CARBOHYDRATES	320	211	GRAMS
TOTAL FAT	71	44	GRAMS
TOTAL SATURATED FAT	32	20	GRAMS
TOTAL CHOLESTEROL	124	78	MILLIGRAMS
TOTAL SODIUM	4280	3208	MILLIGRAMS
TOTAL FIBRE	8	5	GRAMS
% CALORIES FROM FAT	30	29	

Ethiopian Honey Bread

This African bread is complex to make by hand, but it works quite well in this version, adapted for the bread machine. It has a spicy, somewhat sweet taste.

1½-pound

1½ teaspoons active dry yeast

3¼ cups all-purpose flour

1 teaspoon salt

½ teaspoon ground cloves

½ teaspoon ground cinnamon

2 teaspoons ground coriander

3½ tablespoons butter

4½ ounces warm milk

6 tablespoons honey

1 egg

2 tablespoons warm water

1-pound

1 teaspoon active dry yeast

2¼ cups all-purpose flour

½ teaspoon salt

½ teaspoon ground cloves

½ teaspoon ground cinnamon

1½ teaspoons ground coriander

2½ tablespoons butter

3 ounces warm milk

4 tablespoons honey

1 egg

1½ tablespoons warm water

Note:

For Panasonic/National machines, use 3 teaspoons of yeast for the 1½-pound loaf.

NUTRITIONAL ANALYSIS			
	1½-POUND	1-POUND	
TOTAL CALORIES	2478	1738	
TOTAL PROTEIN	66	48	GRAMS
TOTAL CARBOHYDRATES	431	297	GRAMS
TOTAL FAT	55	40	GRAMS
TOTAL SATURATED FAT	28	21	GRAMS
TOTAL CHOLESTEROL	327	294	MILLIGRAMS
TOTAL SODIUM	2279	1186	MILLIGRAMS
TOTAL FIBRE	9	6	GRAMS
% CALORIES FROM FAT	20	21	

Ethiopian Spice Bread

The distinct and unusual blend of spices in this bread make it a great choice with soups or salads.

1½-pound

1½ teaspoons active dry yeast

3 cups all-purpose flour

½ teaspoon paprika

½ teaspoon salt

½ teaspoon ground cardamom

1 tablespoon ground coriander

½ teaspoon garlic salt

1½ teaspoons dried onion

1 teaspoon hot sauce (red pepper)

5½ tablespoons butter

7 ounces warm water

1-pound

1 teaspoon active dry yeast

2 cups all-purpose flour

½ teaspoon paprika

½ teaspoon salt

½ teaspoon ground cardamom

2 teaspoons ground coriander

½ teaspoon garlic salt

1 teaspoon dried onion

½ teaspoon hot sauce (red pepper)

3½ tablespoons butter

4½ ounces warm water

Notes:

1. For Panasonic/National machines, use 3 teaspoons of yeast for the 1½-pound loaf.
2. For DAK/Welbilt machines, use 2 additional tablespoons of warm water for the 1½-pound loaf.

NUTRITIONAL ANALYSIS			
	1½-POUND	1-POUND	
TOTAL CALORIES	2072	1365	
TOTAL PROTEIN	52	35	GRAMS
TOTAL CARBOHYDRATES	305	204	GRAMS
TOTAL FAT	71	45	GRAMS
TOTAL SATURATED FAT	40	26	GRAMS
TOTAL CHOLESTEROL	171	109	MILLIGRAMS
TOTAL SODIUM	2239	2189	MILLIGRAMS
TOTAL FIBRE	8	6	GRAMS
% CALORIES FROM FAT	31	30	

Georgian Cheese Bread

This favorite from the Caucasus is a very rich, flaky textured bread. The dough is made in the bread machine and then removed to be flattened, filled, and baked in the oven.

1½-pound

1½ teaspoons active dry yeast

1 tablespoon sugar

3 cups all-purpose flour

2 teaspoons salt

8 tablespoons butter

¾ cup warm milk

Filling(do not place in bread machine):

1¼ cup mozzarella or cheddar cheese (shredded)

1 egg

2½ tablespoons butter

1-pound

1 teaspoon active dry yeast

2 teaspoons sugar

2 cups all-purpose flour

1½ teaspoons salt

5½ tablespoons butter

½ cup warm milk

¾ cup mozzarella or cheddar cheese (shredded)

1 egg

1½ tablespoons butter

Notes:

1. For Panasonic/National machines, use 3 teaspoons of yeast for the 1½-pound loaf.
2. Use the dough cycle and remove the dough when complete. Finish the bread according to the baking instructions below.

Instructions for baking:

Remove the dough from the bread machine. Flatten the dough into a round shape, about ¼ inch thick. Place the dough on a greased pie plate in much the same manner as you would a piecrust. Gently press the dough down into the bottom of the pie plate, shaping it to conform to the contour of the plate. Prepare the filling, mix it well, and spoon it into the crust in the pie plate. Fold the remaining crust over the top of the filling until the filling is completely covered. Let rise 15–20 minutes in a warm location (cover with a towel or cloth). Bake in a preheated 375 °F oven for 60 minutes or until brown on top.

NUTRITIONAL ANALYSIS			
	1½-POUND	1-POUND	
TOTAL CALORIES	3312	2195	
TOTAL PROTEIN	99	66	GRAMS
TOTAL CARBOHYDRATES	323	215	GRAMS
TOTAL FAT	181	119	GRAMS
TOTAL SATURATED FAT	108	71	GRAMS
TOTAL CHOLESTEROL	695	524	MILLIGRAMS
TOTAL SODIUM	5314	3861	MILLIGRAMS
TOTAL FIBRE	7	4	GRAMS
% CALORIES FROM FAT	40	49	

WESTERN EUROPEAN BREADS

Germany, Austria, and France are represented by breads in this section. You will find a great variety of recipes, including everything from soft, sweet, white breads to dense, sour ryes.

Feather Bread

This French recipe gets its name from the airy loaf it produces. Experiment with the amount of yeast to get just the lightness you desire. Try the 1-pound loaf first to make sure the volume of the larger loaf won't overflow your machine.

1½-pound

2 teaspoons active dry yeast

1½ teaspoons sugar

3 cups bread flour

1½ teaspoons salt

3 tablespoons butter

1 cup warm water

1-pound

1½ teaspoons active dry yeast

1 teaspoon sugar

2 cups bread flour

1 teaspoon salt

2 tablespoons butter

5 ounces warm water

Notes:
1. For Panasonic/National machines, use 4 teaspoons of yeast for the 1½-pound loaf.
2. For DAK/Welbilt machines, use 2 additional tablespoons of warm water for the 1½-pound loaf.

NUTRITIONAL ANALYSIS			
	1½-POUND	1-POUND	
TOTAL CALORIES	1822	1216	
TOTAL PROTEIN	52	35	GRAMS
TOTAL CARBOHYDRATES	306	204	GRAMS
TOTAL FAT	41	28	GRAMS
TOTAL SATURATED FAT	22	15	GRAMS
TOTAL CHOLESTEROL	93	62	MILLIGRAMS
TOTAL SODIUM	3210	2140	MILLIGRAMS
TOTAL FIBRE	7	5	GRAMS
% CALORIES FROM FAT	20	20	

Hausbrot

Hausbrot could be any homemade bread. This loaf combines a light wheat and rye flavor and texture with a touch of potato for a basic, traditional German bread.

1½-pound

2 teaspoons active dry yeast

1½ tablespoons gluten powder

1 teaspoon caraway seed

1½ cups bread flour

1½ tablespoons sugar

¾ cup whole-wheat flour

½ teaspoon salt

¾ cup rye flour

¾ cup potato flakes or buds

10 ounces warm water

1-pound

1½ teaspoons active dry yeast

1 tablespoon gluten powder

½ teaspoon caraway seed

1 cup bread flour

1 tablespoon sugar

½ cup whole-wheat flour

½ teaspoon salt

½ cup rye flour

½ cup potato flakes or buds

7 ounces warm water

Note:

For Panasonic/National machines, use 3 teaspoons of yeast for the 1½-pound loaf.

NUTRITIONAL ANALYSIS			
	1½-POUND	1-POUND	
TOTAL CALORIES	1688	1126	
TOTAL PROTEIN	62	41	GRAMS
TOTAL CARBOHYDRATES	329	219	GRAMS
TOTAL FAT	16	11	GRAMS
TOTAL SATURATED FAT	1	1	GRAMS
TOTAL CHOLESTEROL	0	0	MILLIGRAMS
TOTAL SODIUM	1615	1432	MILLIGRAMS
TOTAL FIBRE	27	18	GRAMS
% CALORIES FROM FAT	9	9	

Heidelberg Rye Bread

Although similar to German country-rye bread, this bread has a slightly different combination of ingredients.

1½-pound

3 teaspoons active dry yeast

½ tablespoon caraway seeds

1½ cups bread flour

½ tablespoon salt

½ tablespoon sugar

2 tablespoons unsweetened cocoa

1½ cups rye flour

1 tablespoon butter

2½ tablespoons molasses

1 cup warm water

3 tablespoons gluten (optional)

1-pound

2 teaspoons active dry yeast

1 teaspoon caraway seeds

1 cup bread flour

1 teaspoon salt

1 teaspoon sugar

4 teaspoons unsweetened cocoa

1 cup rye flour

1 tablespoon butter

1½ tablespoons molasses

5½ ounces warm water

2 tablespoons gluten (optional)

Notes:
1. For Panasonic/National machines, use 4 teaspoons of yeast for the 1½-pound loaf.
2. For DAK/Welbilt machines, use 2 additional tablespoons of warm water for the 1½-pound loaf.

NUTRITIONAL ANALYSIS			
	1½-POUND	1-POUND	
TOTAL CALORIES	1715	1166	
TOTAL PROTEIN	58	39	GRAMS
TOTAL CARBOHYDRATES	332	219	GRAMS
TOTAL FAT	22	19	GRAMS
TOTAL SATURATED FAT	8	8	GRAMS
TOTAL CHOLESTEROL	31	31	MILLIGRAMS
TOTAL SODIUM	3248	2163	MILLIGRAMS
TOTAL FIBRE	8	5	GRAMS
% CALORIES FROM FAT	12	14	

Kugelhopf Bread

A slightly sweet white bread, *Kugelhopf* is an excellent breakfast bread. It is particularly good spread with jam or jelly.

1½-pound

1½ teaspoons active dry yeast

½ teaspoon dried lemon peel

3 cups + 2 tablespoons bread flour

½ teaspoon salt

3 tablespoons sugar

2 eggs

4 tablespoons butter

2 ounces warm water

½ cup warm milk

¼ cup slivered almonds

½ cup currants

1-pound

1 teaspoon active dry yeast

½ teaspoon dried lemon peel

2 cups + 2 tablespoons bread flour

½ teaspoon salt

2 tablespoons sugar

1 egg

2½ tablespoons butter

2 ounces warm water

2 ounces warm milk

2 tablespoons slivered almonds

¼ cup currants

Notes:

1. For Panasonic/National machines, use 3 teaspoons of yeast for the 1½-pound loaf.
2. Almonds and currants may be added at the mix beep (if your machine is equipped with one). They may also be added at the beginning with the other ingredients.

NUTRITIONAL ANALYSIS			
	1½-POUND	1-POUND	
TOTAL CALORIES	2706	1706	
TOTAL PROTEIN	76	48	GRAMS
TOTAL CARBOHYDRATES	418	271	GRAMS
TOTAL FAT	83	49	GRAMS
TOTAL SATURATED FAT	35	21	GRAMS
TOTAL CHOLESTEROL	555	293	MILLIGRAMS
TOTAL SODIUM	1278	1174	MILLIGRAMS
TOTAL FIBRE	12	7	GRAMS
% CALORIES FROM FAT	28	26	

La Fouace

This French hearth bread is a hearty white bread with a slight wheat flavor. Toasting it brings out the walnut and wheat flavors.

1½-pound

1½ teaspoons active dry yeast

¼ cup whole-wheat flour

6 tablespoons chopped walnuts

2 teaspoons salt

2¾ cups bread flour

4 tablespoons butter

6 ounces warm milk

3 ounces warm water

1-pound

1 teaspoon active dry yeast

3 tablespoons whole-wheat flour

4 tablespoons chopped walnuts

1½ teaspoons salt

1¾ cups + 2 tablespoons bread flour

2½ tablespoons butter

4 ounces warm milk

2 ounces warm water

Note:

For Panasonic/National machines, use 3 teaspoons of yeast for the 1½-pound loaf.

NUTRITIONAL ANALYSIS			
	1½-POUND	1-POUND	
TOTAL CALORIES	2239	1483	
TOTAL PROTEIN	64	43	GRAMS
TOTAL CARBOHYDRATES	314	210	GRAMS
TOTAL FAT	82	53	GRAMS
TOTAL SATURATED FAT	33	21	GRAMS
TOTAL CHOLESTEROL	132	83	MILLIGRAMS
TOTAL SODIUM	4372	3270	MILLIGRAMS
TOTAL FIBRE	12	8	GRAMS
% CALORIES FROM FAT	33	32	

Milk Bread

This traditional Austrian bread is most often baked in a braided loaf, but the flavor, aroma, and texture come through in the bread machine, too.

1½-pound

1½ teaspoons active dry yeast

1 teaspoon ground caraway

1 teaspoon anise seed

3 cups bread flour

½ teaspoon salt

2 tablespoons sugar

6 tablespoons butter

8 ounces warm milk

1-pound

1 teaspoon active dry yeast

½ teaspoon ground caraway

½ teaspoon anise seed

2 cups bread flour

½ teaspoon salt

4 teaspoons sugar

4 tablespoons butter

5 ounces warm milk

Note:

For Panasonic/National machines, use 3 teaspoons of yeast for the 1½-pound loaf.

NUTRITIONAL ANALYSIS			
	1½-POUND	1-POUND	
TOTAL CALORIES	2297	1526	
TOTAL PROTEIN	60	39	GRAMS
TOTAL CARBOHYDRATES	336	223	GRAMS
TOTAL FAT	78	52	GRAMS
TOTAL SATURATED FAT	45	30	GRAMS
TOTAL CHOLESTEROL	196	130	MILLIGRAMS
TOTAL SODIUM	1203	1152	MILLIGRAMS
TOTAL FIBRE	7	5	GRAMS
% CALORIES FROM FAT	31	31	

Muenster-Cheese Loaf

Fresh Muenster cheese characterizes this rich white bread. It makes an outstanding sandwich.

1½-pound

1½ teaspoons active dry yeast

1 teaspoon sugar

3 cups + 3 tablespoons bread flour

2 teaspoons salt

½ cup shredded Muenster cheese

2 eggs

1½ tablespoons butter

½ cup plain yogurt

1-pound

1 teaspoon active dry yeast

½ teaspoon sugar

2 cups + 2 tablespoons bread flour

1½ teaspoons salt

¼ cup shredded Muenster cheese

2 eggs

1 tablespoon butter

¼ cup plain yogurt

Note:

For Panasonic/National machines, use 3 teaspoons of yeast for the 1½-pound loaf.

NUTRITIONAL ANALYSIS			
	1½-POUND	1-POUND	
TOTAL CALORIES	2203	1466	
TOTAL PROTEIN	87	59	GRAMS
TOTAL CARBOHYDRATES	332	220	GRAMS
TOTAL FAT	55	37	GRAMS
TOTAL SATURATED FAT	28	17	GRAMS
TOTAL CHOLESTEROL	539	490	MILLIGRAMS
TOTAL SODIUM	4830	3546	MILLIGRAMS
TOTAL FIBRE	7	5	GRAMS
% CALORIES FROM FAT	23	22	

Soft Pumpernickel Bread

The addition of wheat flour softens this traditional rye bread, giving it a higher rise and a softer texture than pure rye bread.

1½-pound

2 teaspoons active dry yeast

¾ cup whole-wheat flour

1½ cups bread flour

¾ cup rye flour

2 teaspoons salt

1 tablespoon butter

1½ tablespoons molasses

3 tablespoons honey

1 cup warm water

1-pound

1½ teaspoons active dry yeast

½ cup whole-wheat flour

1 cup bread flour

½ cup rye flour

1½ teaspoons salt

½ tablespoon butter

1 tablespoon molasses

1½ tablespoons honey

6 ounces warm water

Note:

For Panasonic/National machines, use 3 teaspoons of yeast for the 1½-pound loaf.

NUTRITIONAL ANALYSIS			
	1½-POUND	1-POUND	
TOTAL CALORIES	1712	1096	
TOTAL PROTEIN	45	30	GRAMS
TOTAL CARBOHYDRATES	347	223	GRAMS
TOTAL FAT	18	10	GRAMS
TOTAL SATURATED FAT	8	4	GRAMS
TOTAL CHOLESTEROL	31	16	MILLIGRAMS
TOTAL SODIUM	4295	3219	MILLIGRAMS
TOTAL FIBRE	26	18	GRAMS
% CALORIES FROM FAT	9	8	

Sour Rye Bread

Although you can use various types of starter for this recipe, sourdough starter works well and is used here. See page 44 for the sourdough starter recipe. This is a very densely textured excellent-tasting, rye bread.

1½-pound

1½ teaspoons active dry yeast

¾ cup sourdough starter batter

1½ cups bread flour

1½ cups rye flour

1½ teaspoons salt

7½ ounces warm water

2 tablespoons molasses

1-pound

1 teaspoon active dry yeast

½ cup sourdough starter batter

1 cup bread flour

1 cup rye flour

1 teaspoon salt

4½ ounces warm water

4 teaspoons molasses

Notes:

1. For Panasonic/National machines, use 3 teaspoons of yeast for the 1½-pound loaf.
2. For DAK/Welbilt machines, use 2 additional tablespoons of warm water for the 1½-pound loaf.

Instructions for baking:

Mix ingredients through the end of the mix cycle. Turn off the bread machine and reset it to start a complete cycle in 4–5 hours (completion in 8–9 hours). The long first rise gives the sourdough and the yeast time to interact and to proof.

NUTRITIONAL ANALYSIS			
	1½-POUND	1-POUND	
TOTAL CALORIES	1867	1245	
TOTAL PROTEIN	65	44	GRAMS
TOTAL CARBOHYDRATES	385	257	GRAMS
TOTAL FAT	10	7	GRAMS
TOTAL SATURATED FAT	1	1	GRAMS
TOTAL CHOLESTEROL	0	0	MILLIGRAMS
TOTAL SODIUM	3237	2158	MILLIGRAMS
TOTAL FIBRE	8	5	GRAMS
% CALORIES FROM FAT	5	5	

Viennese Hausbrot

This bread is half rye and doesn't rise much (hence the need for extra gluten). The taste and texture are wonderful, particularly if you like rye breads. Add caraway seed, if you like.

1½-pound

2 teaspoons active dry yeast

1 teaspoon anise seed

1½ tablespoons gluten powder

1 tablespoon sugar

1½ cups bread flour

1½ cups rye flour

½ teaspoon salt

¾ cup potato flakes or buds

11 ounces warm water

1-pound

1½ teaspoons active dry yeast

½ teaspoon anise seed

1 tablespoon gluten powder

½ tablespoon sugar

1 cup bread flour

1 cup rye flour

½ teaspoon salt

½ cup potato flakes or buds

1 cup warm water

Note:

For Panasonic/National machines, use 3½ teaspoons of yeast for the 1½-pound loaf.

NUTRITIONAL ANALYSIS			
	1½-POUND	1-POUND	
TOTAL CALORIES	1634	1083	
TOTAL PROTEIN	55	37	GRAMS
TOTAL CARBOHYDRATES	318	210	GRAMS
TOTAL FAT	16	10	GRAMS
TOTAL SATURATED FAT	1	0	GRAMS
TOTAL CHOLESTEROL	0	0	MILLIGRAMS
TOTAL SODIUM	1615	1432	MILLIGRAMS
TOTAL FIBRE	27	18	GRAMS
% CALORIES FROM FAT	9	9	

Viennese Potato Bread (Erdapfelbrot)

This simple white bread is rich with cream and butter, with a somewhat sweet taste provided by the raisins.

1½-pound

1½ teaspoons active dry yeast

3 cups bread flour

2 tablespoons raisins

¾ cup potato flakes or buds

½ cup whipping cream

2 tablespoons butter

7 ounces warm water

1-pound

1 teaspoon active dry yeast

2 cups bread flour

4 teaspoons raisins

½ cup potato flakes or buds

2½ ounces whipping cream

1½ tablespoons butter

4½ ounces warm water

Note:

For Panasonic/National machines, use 3 teaspoons of yeast for the 1½-pound loaf.

NUTRITIONAL ANALYSIS			
	1½-POUND	1-POUND	
TOTAL CALORIES	2191	1467	
TOTAL PROTEIN	60	40	GRAMS
TOTAL CARBOHYDRATES	344	229	GRAMS
TOTAL FAT	63	43	GRAMS
TOTAL SATURATED FAT	30	21	GRAMS
TOTAL CHOLESTEROL	113	78	MILLIGRAMS
TOTAL SODIUM	614	407	MILLIGRAMS
TOTAL FIBRE	8	5	GRAMS
% CALORIES FROM FAT	26	26	

Viennese Striezel Bread

Striezel bread is braided, but the texture and flavor develop well in the bread machine. This recipe is a plain *striezel*, using only basic ingredients.

1½-pound

1½ teaspoons active dry yeast

4 tablespoons sugar

2½ cups bread flour

½ teaspoon salt

¾ cup barley flour

3 tablespoons butter

1 egg

1 cup warm milk

1-pound

1 teaspoon active dry yeast

2½ tablespoons sugar

1¾ cups bread flour

½ teaspoon salt

½ cup barley flour

2 tablespoons butter

1 egg

5 ounces warm milk.

Note:

For Panasonic/National machines, use 3 teaspoons of yeast for the 1½-pound loaf.

NUTRITIONAL ANALYSIS			
	1½-POUND	1-POUND	
TOTAL CALORIES	2209	1527	
TOTAL PROTEIN	68	48	GRAMS
TOTAL CARBOHYDRATES	362	248	GRAMS
TOTAL FAT	49	35	GRAMS
TOTAL SATURATED FAT	25	17	GRAMS
TOTAL CHOLESTEROL	316	281	MILLIGRAMS
TOTAL SODIUM	1263	1214	MILLIGRAMS
TOTAL FIBRE	16	11	GRAMS
% CALORIES FROM FAT	20	20	

Viennese Striezel Bread II

A slight variation in texture, and the addition of raisins and almonds, give this version of *striezel* just enough of a sweet flavor to make an excellent breakfast bread.

1½-pound

1½ teaspoons active dry yeast

4 tablespoons sugar

2¾ cups bread flour

¾ cup barley flour

1 teaspoon dried lemon peel

1½ teaspoons raisins

3 tablespoons chopped almonds

½ teaspoon salt

3 tablespoons butter

1 egg

9 ounces warm milk

1-pound

1 teaspoon active dry yeast

2½ tablespoons sugar

2 cups bread flour

½ cup barley flour

½ teaspoon dried lemon peel

1 tablespoon raisins

2 tablespoons chopped almonds

½ teaspoon salt

2 tablespoons butter

1 egg

¾ cup warm milk

Note:

For Panasonic/National machines, use 3 teaspoons of yeast for the 1½-pound loaf.

NUTRITIONAL ANALYSIS			
	1½-POUND	1-POUND	
TOTAL CALORIES	2531	1787	
TOTAL PROTEIN	76	56	GRAMS
TOTAL CARBOHYDRATES	403	284	GRAMS
TOTAL FAT	64	45	GRAMS
TOTAL SATURATED FAT	27	18	GRAMS
TOTAL CHOLESTEROL	317	283	MILLIGRAMS
TOTAL SODIUM	1283	1232	MILLIGRAMS
TOTAL FIBRE	19	13	GRAMS
% CALORIES FROM FAT	23	23	

Vollkornbrot

This compact bread has a distinct wheat flavor.

1½-pound	1-pound
1½ teaspoons active dry yeast	1 teaspoon active dry yeast
2 tablespoons gluten (optional)	1½ tablespoons gluten (optional)
3 cups whole-wheat flour	2 cups whole-wheat flour
½ tablespoon salt	1 teaspoon salt
¼ cup dry milk	2 tablespoons dry milk
¼ teaspoon sugar	¼ teaspoon sugar
1 tablespoon butter	½ tablespoon butter
2 tablespoons dark molasses	1½ tablespoons dark molasses
10 ounces warm water	6½ ounces warm water

Notes:
1. For Panasonic/National machines, use 3 teaspoons of yeast for the 1½-pound loaf.
2. For DAK/Welbilt machines, use 2 additional tablespoons of warm water for the 1½-pound loaf.

NUTRITIONAL ANALYSIS			
	1½-POUND	1-POUND	
TOTAL CALORIES	1537	1006	
TOTAL PROTEIN	59	38	GRAMS
TOTAL CARBOHYDRATES	304	203	GRAMS
TOTAL FAT	18	10	GRAMS
TOTAL SATURATED FAT	8	4	GRAMS
TOTAL CHOLESTEROL	35	18	MILLIGRAMS
TOTAL SODIUM	3359	2221	MILLIGRAMS
TOTAL FIBRE	46	31	GRAMS
% CALORIES FROM FAT	11	9	

Weissbrot mit Kümmel

White bread with caraway is a favorite in Austria and Germany. It is excellent as a sandwich bread.

1½-pound

1½ teaspoons active dry yeast

2 teaspoons caraway seeds

1½ tablespoons sugar

3 cups bread flour

2 teaspoons salt

5 tablespoons butter

1 egg

5 ounces warm milk

2 ounces warm water

1-pound

1 teaspoon active dry yeast

1½ teaspoons caraway seeds

1 tablespoon sugar

2 cups bread flour

1½ teaspoons salt

3 tablespoons butter

1 egg

3 ounces warm milk

1½ ounces warm water

Notes:

1. For Panasonic/National machines, use 3 teaspoons of yeast for the 1½-pound loaf.
2. For DAK/Welbilt machines, use 2 additional tablespoons of warm water for the 1½-pound loaf.

NUTRITIONAL ANALYSIS			
	1½-POUND	1-POUND	
TOTAL CALORIES	2217	1467	
TOTAL PROTEIN	63	44	GRAMS
TOTAL CARBOHYDRATES	328	218	GRAMS
TOTAL FAT	71	45	GRAMS
TOTAL SATURATED FAT	39	24	GRAMS
TOTAL CHOLESTEROL	374	310	MILLIGRAMS
TOTAL SODIUM	4417	3315	MILLIGRAMS
TOTAL FIBRE	7	5	GRAMS
% CALORIES FROM FAT	29	28	

Zeppelin Bread

Similar to French bread, this recipe is typically baked in long loaves that resemble German zeppelin airships. In the bread machine, of course, the shape is different, but the wonderful taste remains the same.

1½-pound

1½ teaspoons active dry yeast

3 cups + 2 tablespoons bread flour

1½ teaspoons salt

½ tablespoon dry milk

¼ teaspoon sugar

1 tablespoon olive oil

9 ounces warm water

1-pound

1 teaspoon active dry yeast

2 cups bread flour

1 teaspoon salt

1 teaspoon dry milk

¼ teaspoon sugar

2 teaspoons olive oil

6 ounces warm water

Notes:

1. For Panasonic/National machines, use 3 teaspoons of yeast for the 1½-pound loaf.
2. For DAK/Welbilt machines, use 2 additional tablespoons of warm water for the 1½-pound loaf.
3. Use the French-bread setting (if your machine is equipped with one).

NUTRITIONAL ANALYSIS			
	1½-POUND	1-POUND	
TOTAL CALORIES	1693	1087	
TOTAL PROTEIN	54	34	GRAMS
TOTAL CARBOHYDRATES	315	202	GRAMS
TOTAL FAT	21	14	GRAMS
TOTAL SATURATED FAT	3	2	GRAMS
TOTAL CHOLESTEROL	1	0	MILLIGRAMS
TOTAL SODIUM	3222	2148	MILLIGRAMS
TOTAL FIBRE	7	4	GRAMS
% CALORIES FROM FAT	11	11	

SCANDINAVIAN AND FINNISH BREADS

The breads in this section are from Denmark, Finland, and Sweden. These countries have a rich tradition of bread baking. You will find these recipes delightfully different from any other breads.

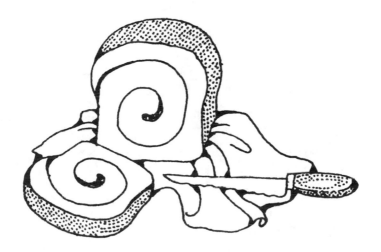

Danish Sour Bread

This dense, whole-grain bread doesn't rise much. It has a hearty, tart flavor. The rice flour called for is generally available in health-food stores.

1½-pound

1½ teaspoons active dry yeast

3 tablespoons gluten (optional)

¾ cup sourdough starter batter

1 teaspoon ground caraway seed

1 teaspoon salt

½ cup rice flour

½ cup rye flour

2 cups whole-wheat flour

9 ounces warm water

3 tablespoons butter

1-pound

1 teaspoon active dry yeast

2 tablespoons gluten (optional)

½ cup sourdough starter batter

½ teaspoon ground caraway seed

½ teaspoon salt

¼ cup rice flour

¼ cup rye flour

1½ cups whole-wheat flour

6 ounces warm water

2 tablespoons butter

Notes:

1. For Panasonic/National machines, use 3 teaspoons of yeast for the 1½-pound loaf.
2. For DAK/Welbilt machines, use 2 additional tablespoons of warm water for the 1½-pound loaf.

NUTRITIONAL ANALYSIS			
	1½-POUND	1-POUND	
TOTAL CALORIES	1918	1276	
TOTAL PROTEIN	65	43	GRAMS
TOTAL CARBOHYDRATES	339	226	GRAMS
TOTAL FAT	44	29	GRAMS
TOTAL SATURATED FAT	23	15	GRAMS
TOTAL CHOLESTEROL	93	62	MILLIGRAMS
TOTAL SODIUM	2142	1073	MILLIGRAMS
TOTAL FIBRE	35	25	GRAMS
% CALORIES FROM FAT	21	21	

Finnish Cardamom Loaf

Cardamom, the seed of an East Indian herb, lightly flavors this loaf of white bread, which is particularly good for breakfast, especially if eaten warm.

1½-pound

1½ teaspoons active dry yeast

2½ tablespoons sugar

1 teaspoon cardamom

3 cups + 3 tablespoons bread flour

1 teaspoon salt

1 egg

2 tablespoons butter

1 cup warm water

1-pound

1 teaspoon active dry yeast

1½ tablespoons sugar

½ teaspoon cardamom

2 cups + 2 tablespoons bread flour

½ teaspoon salt

1 egg

1½ tablespoons butter

5 ounces warm water

Note:

For Panasonic/National machines, use 3 teaspoons of yeast for the 1½-pound loaf.

NUTRITIONAL ANALYSIS			
	1½-POUND	1-POUND	
TOTAL CALORIES	1078	1353	
TOTAL PROTEIN	00	42	GRAMS
TOTAL CARBOHYDRATES	349	231	GRAMS
TOTAL FAT	35	27	GRAMS
TOTAL SATURATED FAT	17	13	GRAMS
TOTAL CHOLESTEROL	275	260	MILLIGRAMS
TOTAL SODIUM	2205	1136	MILLIGRAMS
TOTAL FIBRE	7	5	GRAMS
% CALORIES FROM FAT	16	18	

Finnish Easter-Crown Bread

Traditionally, Finns bake this bread in the spring to celebrate the arrival of the new calves and the abundance of dairy products. It is delicious with cream cheese or other soft, spreadable cheeses.

1½-pound

1½ teaspoons active dry yeast

¾ cup rye flour

¼ teaspoon dried orange peel

¼ teaspoon dried lemon peel

½ teaspoon cardamom

½ teaspoon salt

6 tablespoons sugar

2 cups all-purpose flour

1 egg yolk

4½ tablespoons butter

1 ounce warm water

6 ounces whipping cream

4 tablespoons chopped almonds

¼ cup raisins

1-pound

1 teaspoon active dry yeast

½ cup rye flour

¼ teaspoon dried orange peel

¼ teaspoon dried lemon peel

½ teaspoon cardamom

½ teaspoon salt

4 tablespoons sugar

1½ cups all-purpose flour

1 egg yolk

3 tablespoons butter

1 ounce warm water

4 ounces whipping cream

2½ tablespoons chopped almonds

2 tablespoons raisins

Notes:

1. For Panasonic/National machines, use 3 teaspoons of yeast for the 1½-pound loaf.
2. For DAK/Welbilt machines, use 2 additional tablespoons of warm water for the 1½-pound loaf.
3. Add the raisins and almonds at the mix-cycle beep or at the end of the initial mix cycle, if your machine is not equipped with an automatic mix cycle.

NUTRITIONAL ANALYSIS			
	1½-POUND	1-POUND	
TOTAL CALORIES	2784	1937	
TOTAL PROTEIN	65	48	GRAMS
TOTAL CARBOHYDRATES	380	265	GRAMS
TOTAL FAT	118	80	GRAMS
TOTAL SATURATED FAT	59	40	GRAMS
TOTAL CHOLESTEROL	429	357	MILLIGRAMS

TOTAL SODIUM	1241	1203	MILLIGRAMS
TOTAL FIBRE	9	6	GRAMS
% CALORIES FROM FAT	38	37	

Finnish Rye Bread

A traditional rye, this bread is simple and tasty. The combination of bread flour and rye flour helps to give it a wonderful texture.

1½-pound

1½ teaspoons active dry yeast

1½ cups bread flour

1½ cups rye flour

1½ teaspoons salt

2 tablespoons sugar

2 tablespoons butter

1 cup warm water

1-pound

1 teaspoon active dry yeast

1 cup bread flour

1 cup rye flour

1 teaspoon salt

4 teaspoons sugar

1½ tablespoons butter

5½ ounces warm water

Notes:

1. For Panasonic/National machines, use 3 teaspoons of yeast for the 1½-pound loaf.
2. For DAK/Welbilt machines, use 2 additional tablespoons of warm water for the 1½-pound loaf.

NUTRITIONAL ANALYSIS		
	1½-POUND	1-POUND	
TOTAL CALORIES	1606	1087	
TOTAL PROTEIN	39	26	GRAMS
TOTAL CARBOHYDRATES	297	198	GRAMS
TOTAL FAT	29	21	GRAMS
TOTAL SATURATED FAT	15	11	GRAMS
TOTAL CHOLESTEROL	62	47	MILLIGRAMS
TOTAL SODIUM	3208	2139	MILLIGRAMS
TOTAL FIBRE	26	17	GRAMS
% CALORIES FROM FAT	16	17	

Rieska Bread

Rieska bread is normally baked in flat cakes using pure barley flour. This recipe produces some of the same flavor in a yeast-based, fully baked loaf.

1½-pound

1½ teaspoons active dry yeast

1 tablespoon sugar

1½ cups barley flour

1½ cups bread flour

1 teaspoon salt

3 tablespoons butter

9 ounces half-and-half

1-pound

1 teaspoon active dry yeast

2 teaspoons sugar

1 cup barley flour

1 cup bread flour

¾ teaspoon salt

2 tablespoons butter

6 ounces half-and-half

Notes:
1. For Panasonic/National machines, use 3 teaspoons of yeast for the 1½-pound loaf.
2. For DAK/Welbilt machines, use 2 additional tablespoons of warm water for the 1½-pound loaf.

NUTRITIONAL ANALYSIS			
	1½-POUND	1-POUND	
TOTAL CALORIES	2254	1502	
TOTAL PROTEIN	56	37	GRAMS
TOTAL CARBOHYDRATES	278	186	GRAMS
TOTAL FAT	95	63	GRAMS
TOTAL SATURATED FAT	56	37	GRAMS
TOTAL CHOLESTEROL	208	139	MILLIGRAMS
TOTAL SODIUM	2281	1699	MILLIGRAMS
TOTAL FIBRE	25	17	GRAMS
% CALORIES FROM FAT	38	38	

Rieska Bread II

This recipe lets you mix the dough in your bread machine and then bake the bread in your oven. The result is an authentically shaped and flavored loaf.

1½-pound

3 teaspoons baking powder

1½ teaspoons salt

2 tablespoons sugar

3 cups barley flour

9 ounces cream

3 tablespoons butter

1-pound

2 teaspoons baking powder

1 teaspoon salt

4 teaspoons sugar

2 cups barley flour

6 ounces cream

2 tablespoons butter

Baking instructions:

Remove the dough from the bread machine after the mixing is completed. Flour your hands and form the dough into a ball. Place the dough ball on a greased cookie sheet and flatten it until it is about ½ inch thick. Use a fork to poke holes in the surface of the dough.

Bake in a preheated, 450 °F oven until it is crisp and golden brown. To serve, cut the loaf into wedges while it is still hot. Butter it liberally.

NUTRITIONAL ANALYSIS			
	1½-POUND	1-POUND	
TOTAL CALORIES	2147	1431	
TOTAL PROTEIN	51	34	GRAMS
TOTAL CARBOHYDRATES	245	163	GRAMS
TOTAL FAT	94	63	GRAMS
TOTAL SATURATED FAT	55	37	GRAMS
TOTAL CHOLESTEROL	208	139	MILLIGRAMS
TOTAL SODIUM	3345	2230	MILLIGRAMS
TOTAL FIBRE	43	29	GRAMS
% CALORIES FROM FAT	40	40	

Suomalaisleipaa Bread

Rye grain grows well in Finland's cold climate. This bread combines rye flour and brown sugar to create a loaf that's deep brown in color. It's great served warm with fresh butter.

1½-pound

1½ teaspoons active dry yeast

1¾ cups bread flour

1½ teaspoons salt

1½ tablespoons brown sugar

1½ cups rye flour

1 tablespoon butter

9 ounces warm water

1-pound

1 teaspoon active dry yeast

1 cup + 2 tablespoons bread flour

1 teaspoon salt

1 tablespoon brown sugar

1 cup rye flour

½ tablespoon butter

6 ounces warm water

Notes:
1. For Panasonic/National machines, use 3 teaspoons of yeast for the 1½-pound loaf.
2. For DAK/Welbilt machines, use 2 additional tablespoons of warm water for the 1½-pound loaf.

NUTRITIONAL ANALYSIS			
	1½-POUND	1-POUND	
TOTAL CALORIES	1676	1082	
TOTAL PROTEIN	57	38	GRAMS
TOTAL CARBOHYDRATES	327	215	GRAMS
TOTAL FAT	21	12	GRAMS
TOTAL SATURATED FAT	8	4	GRAMS
TOTAL CHOLESTEROL	31	16	MILLIGRAMS
TOTAL SODIUM	3213	2142	MILLIGRAMS
TOTAL FIBRE	7	5	GRAMS
% CALORIES FROM FAT	11	10	

Swedish Caraway Bread

Caraway and orange are the predominant flavors of this delightful white bread. It is fantastic for sandwiches, particularly with either tuna salad or cheese.

1½-pound

1½ teaspoons active dry yeast

1½ teaspoon caraway seeds

3 cups bread flour

1½ teaspoons salt

1½ teaspoons dried orange peel

3 tablespoons brown sugar

1½ tablespoons butter

9 ounces warm water

1-pound

1 teaspoon active dry yeast

1 teaspoon caraway seeds

2 cups bread flour

1 teaspoon salt

1 teaspoon dried orange peel

2 tablespoons brown sugar

1 tablespoon butter

6 ounces warm water

Note:

For Panasonic/National machines, use 3 teaspoons of yeast for the 1½-pound loaf.

NUTRITIONAL ANALYSIS			
	1½-POUND	1-POUND	
TOTAL CALORIES	1799	1199	
TOTAL PROTEIN	51	34	GRAMS
TOTAL CARBOHYDRATES	339	226	GRAMS
TOTAL FAT	24	16	GRAMS
TOTAL SATURATED FAT	12	8	GRAMS
TOTAL CHOLESTEROL	47	31	MILLIGRAMS
TOTAL SODIUM	3219	2146	MILLIGRAMS
TOTAL FIBRE	7	4	GRAMS
% CALORIES FROM FAT	12	12	

EASTERN EUROPEAN BREADS

Eastern Europe is famous for its wide variety of breads. This section includes breads from Bohemia, Hungary, and Russia. Rye, which grows well in cold climates, is a staple grain in this area and is included in many different recipes.

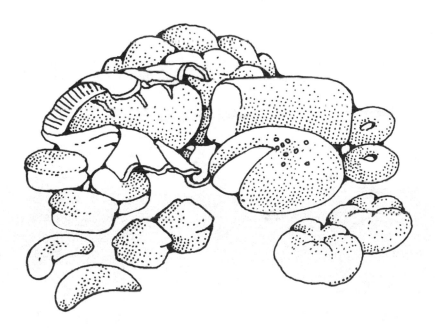

Bohemian Christmas Bread

This delightful bread is great for parties and celebrations. The raisins and nuts give it a festive flavor and texture that's hard to beat. Because this bread is an extremely high riser, a 1-pound loaf will easily fill a large bread-machine bucket. Test the small recipe first to see how the loaf rises in your machine.

1½-pound

1½ teaspoons active dry yeast

3 cups bread flour

1 teaspoon dried lemon peel

1½ teaspoons salt

3½ tablespoons sugar

1 egg

2 tablespoons butter

6 ounces warm milk

2 ounces warm water

4½ tablespoons chopped almonds

3½ tablespoons raisins

1-pound

1 teaspoon active dry yeast

2 cups bread flour

½ teaspoon dried lemon peel

1 teaspoon salt

2½ tablespoons sugar

1 egg

1½ tablespoons butter

½ cup warm milk

1½ ounces warm water

3 tablespoons chopped almonds

2½ tablespoons raisins

Notes:
1. For Panasonic/National machines, use 3 teaspoons of yeast for the 1½-pound loaf.
2. If your machine has a mix cycle, the almonds and raisins can be added at the beginning or at the mix beep. They can also be added towards the end of the mixing process.

NUTRITIONAL ANALYSIS			
	1½-POUND	1-POUND	
TOTAL CALORIES	2320	1600	
TOTAL PROTEIN	69	48	GRAMS
TOTAL CARBOHYDRATES	382	258	GRAMS
TOTAL FAT	58	42	GRAMS
TOTAL SATURATED FAT	20	15	GRAMS
TOTAL CHOLESTEROL	283	265	MILLIGRAMS
TOTAL SODIUM	3371	2268	MILLIGRAMS
TOTAL FIBRE	10	7	GRAMS
% CALORIES FROM FAT	22	24	

Bohemian Houska Bread

A high-rising, airy loaf, this bread is best when cut into thick slices and eaten with cream cheese or butter. Try the small recipe first to make sure you don't overflow your bread bucket.

1½-pound

1 teaspoon active dry yeast

3 cups + 2 tablespoons bread flour

½ teaspoon salt

2 teaspoons sugar

2 ounces warm water

1 egg

3 tablespoons olive oil

6 ounces warm milk

3 tablespoons chopped almonds

4 tablespoons raisins

1-pound

½ teaspoon active dry yeast

2 cups + 1 tablespoon bread flour

½ teaspoon salt

1½ teaspoons sugar

1 ounce warm water

1 egg

2 tablespoons olive oil

½ cup warm milk

2 tablespoons chopped almonds

2½ tablespoons raisins

Notes:

1. For Panasonic/National machines, use 2 teaspoons of yeast for the 1½-pound loaf.
2. You can use the mix cycle (if your machine has one) and add the raisins and almonds at the beep. You can also add them towards the end of the initial mix cycle.

NUTRITIONAL ANALYSIS			
	1½-POUND	1-POUND	
TOTAL CALORIES	2346	1576	
TOTAL PROTEIN	69	47	GRAMS
TOTAL CARBOHYDRATES	362	239	GRAMS
TOTAL FAT	69	47	GRAMS
TOTAL SATURATED FAT	10	7	GRAMS
TOTAL CHOLESTEROL	221	218	MILLIGRAMS
TOTAL SODIUM	1236	1200	MILLIGRAMS
TOTAL FIBRE	10	6	GRAMS
% CALORIES FROM FAT	26	27	

Kulich Bread

Also called *Russian Easter Bread*, this bread is very similar to Bohemian Christmas Bread. It is an extremely high riser, so try the small loaf first. A 1-pound loaf can fill a large bread-machine bucket.

1½-pound

1½ teaspoons active dry yeast

1 teaspoon grated lemon peel

¼ cup sugar

3 cups all-purpose flour

1 teaspoon salt

1 egg

2 tablespoons butter

½ cup warm water

5 ounces warm milk

4 tablespoons raisins

4 tablespoons chopped almonds

1-pound

1 teaspoon active dry yeast

½ teaspoon grated lemon peel

3 tablespoons sugar

2 cups all-purpose flour

½ teaspoon salt

1 egg

1½ tablespoons butter

2 ounces warm water

½ cup warm milk

2½ tablespoons raisins

2½ tablespoons chopped almonds

Notes:

1. For Panasonic/National machines, use 3 teaspoons of yeast for the 1½-pound loaf.
2. The raisins and almonds may be added with the other ingredients or you can add them at the beep (if your machine as a mix cycle).

NUTRITIONAL ANALYSIS			
	1½-POUND	1-POUND	
TOTAL CALORIES	2319	1599	
TOTAL PROTEIN	68	48	GRAMS
TOTAL CARBOHYDRATES	389	263	GRAMS
TOTAL FAT	55	40	GRAMS
TOTAL SATURATED FAT	19	15	GRAMS
TOTAL CHOLESTEROL	281	265	MILLIGRAMS
TOTAL SODIUM	2289	1202	MILLIGRAMS
TOTAL FIBRE	10	6	GRAMS
% CALORIES FROM FAT	21	22	

Pusstabrot

Hungarian white bread is light and airy. The fennel and garlic give it a great flavor. It is an excellent sandwich bread.

1½-pound

1½ teaspoons active dry yeast

3 cups bread flour

½ teaspoon garlic salt

1 teaspoon salt

¼ teaspoon fennel seed

5½ teaspoons sugar

1½ tablespoons olive oil

9 ounces warm water

1-pound

1 teaspoon active dry yeast

2 cups bread flour

½ teaspoon garlic salt

½ teaspoon salt

⅛ teaspoon fennel seed

4 teaspoons sugar

1 tablespoon olive oil

6 ounces warm water

Note:

For Panasonic/National machines, use 3 teaspoons of yeast for the 1½-pound loaf.

NUTRITIONAL ANALYSIS			
	1½-POUND	1-POUND	
TOTAL CALORIES	1758	1177	
TOTAL PROTEIN	51	34	GRAMS
TOTAL CARBOHYDRATES	321	216	GRAMS
TOTAL FAT	27	18	GRAMS
TOTAL SATURATED FAT	4	2	GRAMS
TOTAL CHOLESTEROL	0	0	MILLIGRAMS
TOTAL SODIUM	3206	2137	MILLIGRAMS
TOTAL FIBRE	7	4	GRAMS
% CALORIES FROM FAT	14	14	

Pusstabrot II

Here is a slight variation on the previous recipe. The anise seed adds a unique flavor.

1½-pound

1½ teaspoons active dry yeast

¼ teaspoon crushed anise seed

¼ teaspoon crushed fennel seed

1½ tablespoons sugar

3 cups bread flour

1½ teaspoons salt

2 ounces warm milk

1 tablespoon olive oil

7 ounces warm water

1-pound

1 teaspoon active dry yeast

⅛ teaspoon crushed anise seed

⅛ teaspoon crushed fennel seed

1 tablespoon sugar

2 cups bread flour

1 teaspoon salt

1 ounce warm milk

½ tablespoon olive oil

5 ounces warm water

Note:

For Panasonic/National machines, use 3 teaspoons of yeast for the 1½-pound loaf.

NUTRITIONAL ANALYSIS			
	1½-POUND	1-POUND	
TOTAL CALORIES	1713	1117	
TOTAL PROTEIN	53	35	GRAMS
TOTAL CARBOHYDRATES	321	213	GRAMS
TOTAL FAT	21	12	GRAMS
TOTAL SATURATED FAT	3	2	GRAMS
TOTAL CHOLESTEROL	3	1	MILLIGRAMS
TOTAL SODIUM	3238	2153	MILLIGRAMS
TOTAL FIBRE	7	4	GRAMS
% CALORIES FROM FAT	11	10	

LATIN AMERICAN BREAD

Although most Latin American breads are not easily converted for baking in a bread machine, here's one recipe that demonstrates the distinctive nature of Latin American food.

Cuban Bread

Corn, the staple grain of Latin America, is the featured ingredient in this light and tasty bread. It is excellent with any Latin American dish and with foods from the American Southwest. The bread has a somewhat salty taste, so if you'd like less salt, feel free to cut down on the amount of it.

1½-pound

1½ teaspoons active dry yeast

1 tablespoon cornmeal

3 cups all-purpose flour

2 teaspoons salt

½ tablespoon sugar

9 ounces warm water

1-pound

1 teaspoon active dry yeast

½ tablespoon cornmeal

2 cups all-purpose flour

1½ teaspoons salt

1 teaspoon sugar

6 ounces warm water

Note:

For Panasonic/National machines, use 3 teaspoons of yeast for the 1½-pound loaf.

NUTRITIONAL ANALYSIS			
	1½-POUND	1-POUND	
TOTAL CALORIES	1546	1026	
TOTAL PROTEIN	51	34	GRAMS
TOTAL CARBOHYDRATES	311	207	GRAMS
TOTAL FAT	7	5	GRAMS
TOTAL SATURATED FAT	1	1	GRAMS
TOTAL CHOLESTEROL	0	0	MILLIGRAMS
TOTAL SODIUM	4275	3205	MILLIGRAMS
TOTAL FIBRE	7	5	GRAMS
% CALORIES FROM FAT	4	4	

BREADS OF THE BRITISH ISLES

The British Isles offer a wonderful variety of breads.

English Cobblestone Bread

This simple, fine-textured white bread makes excellent sandwiches and toast.

1½-pound

1½ teaspoons active dry yeast

3 cups bread flour

4 tablespoons sugar

1 teaspoon salt

5 tablespoons butter

½ cup warm milk

½ cup warm water

1-pound

1 teaspoon active dry yeast

2 cups bread flour

2½ tablespoons sugar

½ teaspoon salt

3½ tablespoons butter

3 ounces warm milk

2 ounces warm water

Notes:

1. For Panasonic/National machines, use 3 teaspoons of yeast for the 1½-pound loaf.
2. For DAK/Welbilt machines, use 2 additional tablespoons of warm water for the 1½-pound loaf.

NUTRITIONAL ANALYSIS			
	1½-POUND	1-POUND	
TOTAL CALORIES	2231	1500	
TOTAL PROTEIN	55	37	GRAMS
TOTAL CARBOHYDRATES	353	234	GRAMS
TOTAL FAT	65	46	GRAMS
TOTAL SATURATED FAT	37	26	GRAMS
TOTAL CHOLESTEROL	160	112	MILLIGRAMS
TOTAL SODIUM	2206	1121	MILLIGRAMS
TOTAL FIBRE	7	4	GRAMS
% CALORIES FROM FAT	26	27	

English Oatmeal Bread

Oatmeal and whole-wheat flour make this a tasty loaf. It's a great variation on white bread, yet the whole-grain flavors aren't overpowering.

1½-pound

2 teaspoons active dry yeast

1½ cups bread flour

½ cup whole-wheat flour

1½ teaspoons salt

1 cup rolled oats

3 tablespoons butter

3 ounces warm water

7 ounces warm milk

1-pound

1½ teaspoons active dry yeast

1 cup bread flour

¼ cup whole-wheat flour

1 teaspoon salt

¾ cup rolled oats

2 tablespoons butter

2 ounces warm water

5 ounces warm milk

Notes:

1. For Panasonic/National machines, use 3½ teaspoons of yeast for the 1½-pound loaf.
2. For DAK/Welbilt machines, use 2 additional tablespoons of warm water for the 1½-pound loaf.

NUTRITIONAL ANALYSIS			
	1½-POUND	1-POUND	
TOTAL CALORIES	1660	1104	
TOTAL PROTEIN	55	37	GRAMS
TOTAL CARBOHYDRATES	259	170	GRAMS
TOTAL FAT	46	31	GRAMS
TOTAL SATURATED FAT	24	16	GRAMS
TOTAL CHOLESTEROL	102	68	MILLIGRAMS
TOTAL SODIUM	3318	2217	MILLIGRAMS
TOTAL FIBRE	20	13	GRAMS
% CALORIES FROM FAT	25	25	

Irish Barmbrack

Although it doesn't rise much, this dense loaf is very sweet and quite tasty. Barmbrack ("yeast bread") is one of the rare examples of yeast being used in traditional Irish baking.

1½-pound

1½ teaspoons active dry yeast

¾ teaspoon dried lemon peel

¾ teaspoon allspice

1½ teaspoons salt

¾ cup sugar

3 cups bread flour

3½ tablespoons butter

2 ounces warm water

6 ounces warm milk

6 tablespoons seedless raisins

6 tablespoons currants

1-pound

1 teaspoon active dry yeast

½ teaspoon dried lemon peel

½ teaspoon allspice

1 teaspoon salt

½ cup sugar

2 cups bread flour

2½ tablespoons butter

1 ounce warm water

½ cup warm milk

¼ cup seedless raisins

¼ cup currants

Notes:

1. For Panasonic/National machines, use 3 teaspoons of yeast for the 1½-pound loaf.
2. Raisins and currants may be added in the beginning or at the mix beep (if your machine is equipped with one).

NUTRITIONAL ANALYSIS			
	1½-POUND	1-POUND	
TOTAL CALORIES	2765	1883	
TOTAL PROTEIN	60	40	GRAMS
TOTAL CARBOHYDRATES	528	358	GRAMS
TOTAL FAT	49	35	GRAMS
TOTAL SATURATED FAT	27	19	GRAMS
TOTAL CHOLESTEROL	116	83	MILLIGRAMS
TOTAL SODIUM	3314	2210	MILLIGRAMS
TOTAL FIBRE	12	8	GRAMS
% CALORIES FROM FAT	16	17	

Irish Barmbrack II

This variation of Irish Barmbrack features the wonderful flavor of dried fruit.

1½-pound

1½ teaspoons active dry yeast

1 teaspoon dried lemon peel

¼ cup sugar

3½ cups all-purpose flour

½ teaspoon salt

1 egg

½ cup warm milk

3 ounces warm water

3 tablespoons butter

3 tablespoons dried mixed fruit

½ cup currants

1-pound

1 teaspoon active dry yeast

½ teaspoon dried lemon peel

3 tablespoons sugar

2¼ cups + 2 tablespoons all-purpose flour

½ teaspoon salt

1 egg

3 ounces warm milk

2 ounces warm water

2 tablespoons butter

2 tablespoons dried mixed fruit

5 tablespoons currants

Notes:

1. For Panasonic/National machines, use 3 teaspoons of yeast for the 1½-pound loaf.
2. Chop the dried mixed fruit into small pieces before you add them.
3. You may add the dried fruit and currants at the beginning or at the mix beep (if your machine is equipped with one).

NUTRITIONAL ANALYSIS			
	1½-POUND	1-POUND	
TOTAL CALORIES	2651	1824	
TOTAL PROTEIN	73	51	GRAMS
TOTAL CARBOHYDRATES	482	328	GRAMS
TOTAL FAT	49	35	GRAMS
TOTAL SATURATED FAT	25	17	GRAMS
TOTAL CHOLESTEROL	311	279	MILLIGRAMS
TOTAL SODIUM	1215	1191	MILLIGRAMS
TOTAL FIBRE	13	8	GRAMS
% CALORIES FROM FAT	17	17	

Poor Irish Bread

This fairly standard white bread has a texture that's good for sandwiches or morning toast.

1½-pound

1½ teaspoons active dry yeast

2½ tablespoons sugar

3 cups bread flour

1 teaspoon salt

1 tablespoon butter

3 ounces warm milk

6 ounces warm water

1-pound

1 teaspoon active dry yeast

1½ tablespoons sugar

2 cups bread flour

½ teaspoon salt

½ tablespoon butter

2 ounces warm milk

½ cup warm water

Note:

For Panasonic/National machines, use 3 teaspoons of yeast for the 1½-pound loaf.

NUTRITIONAL ANALYSIS			
	1½-POUND	1-POUND	
TOTAL CALORIES	1749	1142	
TOTAL PROTEIN	54	36	GRAMS
TOTAL CARBOHYDRATES	334	220	GRAMS
TOTAL FAT	19	11	GRAMS
TOTAL SATURATED FAT	9	5	GRAMS
TOTAL CHOLESTEROL	35	18	MILLIGRAMS
TOTAL SODIUM	2187	1103	MILLIGRAMS
TOTAL FIBRE	7	4	GRAMS
% CALORIES FROM FAT	10	9	

Sugar Loaf

This interesting sweet bread, a variation on plain white bread, makes a good dessert bread. It is also excellent with jams or jellies. The chunks of sugar melt during the bake cycle, creating pockets of sweetness.

1½-pound

1½ teaspoons active dry yeast

3 cups bread flour

1 teaspoon salt

1 tablespoon sugar

2½ tablespoons dry milk

1½ tablespoons butter

9 ounces warm water

1-pound

1 teaspoon active dry yeast

2 cups bread flour

½ teaspoon salt

2 teaspoons sugar

1½ tablespoons dry milk

1 tablespoon butter

6 ounces warm water

Note:

For Panasonic/National machines, use 3 teaspoons of yeast for the 1½-pound loaf.

Instructions for baking:

Place ½ cup of sugar cubes and ½ tablespoon of cinnamon in a plastic bag. Crush the sugar cubes into coarse powder and shake the bag to mix the sugar with the cinnamon. Add the crushed mixture at the mix beep or towards the end of the mixing cycle.

Watch closely until the mixture is well blended into the dough. Larger pieces may jam the beater and must be released immediately to prevent motor damage. Large chunks may also scratch the surface of your pan. Make sure that none of the chunks is larger than ¹⁄₁₆ inch in diameter.

Alternately, you may use larger chunks of sugar and mix them into the dough by hand, replacing the dough when you are finished. It is not recommended that you use large chunks in the bread-machine mix cycle because of the danger of jamming the machine or scratching the bread bucket.

NUTRITIONAL ANALYSIS			
	1½-POUND	1-POUND	
TOTAL CALORIES	2110	1342	
TOTAL PROTEIN	56	37	GRAMS
TOTAL CARBOHYDRATES	414	260	GRAMS
TOTAL FAT	24	16	GRAMS
TOTAL SATURATED FAT	12	8	GRAMS
TOTAL CHOLESTEROL	49	33	MILLIGRAMS
TOTAL SODIUM	2219	1119	MILLIGRAMS
TOTAL FIBRE	7	4	GRAMS
% CALORIES FROM FAT	10	11	

Yorkshire Spice Bread

A raisin-bread lover's favorite, this makes an excellent breakfast bread.

1½-pound

1½ teaspoons active dry yeast

½ teaspoon cinnamon

2½ cups + 2 tablespoons bread flour

½ teaspoon nutmeg

1 tablespoon dried orange peel

½ cup powdered sugar

1 egg

2 tablespoons olive oil

3 tablespoons butter

½ tablespoon maple syrup

¾ cup warm milk

½ cup raisins

1-pound

1 teaspoon active dry yeast

½ teaspoon cinnamon

1¾ cups bread flour

½ teaspoon nutmeg

2 teaspoons dried orange peel

5 tablespoons powdered sugar

1 egg

4 teaspoons olive oil

2 tablespoons butter

1 teaspoon maple syrup

½ cup warm milk

¼ cup raisins

Notes:

1. For Panasonic/National machines, use 3 teaspoons of yeast for the 1½-pound loaf.
2. You may add the raisins at the beginning or at the mix beep (if your machine has one).

NUTRITIONAL ANALYSIS			
	1½-POUND	1-POUND	
TOTAL CALORIES	2485	1637	
TOTAL PROTEIN	60	41	GRAMS
TOTAL CARBOHYDRATES	397	253	GRAMS
TOTAL FAT	75	52	GRAMS
TOTAL SATURATED FAT	29	20	GRAMS
TOTAL CHOLESTEROL	314	280	MILLIGRAMS
TOTAL SODIUM	180	140	MILLIGRAMS
TOTAL FIBRE	10	6	GRAMS
% CALORIES FROM FAT	27	28	

SPECIAL BREADS

The breads in this section are for special diets. One of the breads is salt-free, one is very low in calories, and the others are baked without yeast. These demonstrate some of the versatility of the bread machine; a little bit of creativity is all that's needed to bake just about any type of bread.

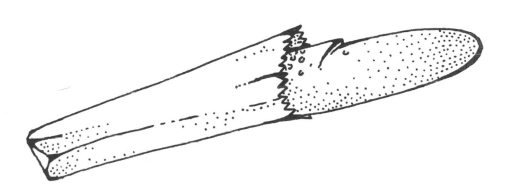

Diet Bread

This bread is very low in calories. An entire 1½-pound loaf has less than 1500 calories, and is almost fat-free.

1½-pound

1½ teaspoons active dry yeast

3 cups bread flour

9 ounces warm water

1-pound

1 teaspoon active dry yeast

2 cups bread flour

6 ounces warm water

Note:

For Panasonic/National machines, use 3 teaspoons of yeast for the 1½-pound loaf.

NUTRITIONAL ANALYSIS			
	1½-POUND	1-POUND	
TOTAL CALORIES	1496	997	
TOTAL PROTEIN	51	34	GRAMS
TOTAL CARBOHYDRATES	300	200	GRAMS
TOTAL FAT	7	5	GRAMS
TOTAL SATURATED FAT	1	1	GRAMS
TOTAL CHOLESTEROL	0	0	MILLIGRAMS
TOTAL SODIUM	8	5	MILLIGRAMS
TOTAL FIBRE	7	4	GRAMS
% CALORIES FROM FAT	4	4	

Salt-Free White Bread

This bread is great for those on a salt-free diet. The only sodium in the recipe comes from the residual sodium in the other ingredients.

1½-pound

1½ teaspoons active dry yeast

3 cups bread flour

1 tablespoon sugar

2 tablespoons olive oil

9 ounces warm water

1-pound

1 teaspoon active dry yeast

2 cups bread flour

2 teaspoons sugar

4 teaspoons olive oil

6 ounces warm water

Note:

For Panasonic/National machines, use 3 teaspoons of yeast for the 1½-pound loaf.

NUTRITIONAL ANALYSIS			
	1½-POUND	1-POUND	
TOTAL CALORIES	1780	1186	
TOTAL PROTEIN	51	34	GRAMS
TOTAL CARBOHYDRATES	311	208	GRAMS
TOTAL FAT	34	23	GRAMS
TOTAL SATURATED FAT	5	3	GRAMS
TOTAL CHOLESTEROL	0	0	MILLIGRAMS
TOTAL SODIUM	8	5	MILLIGRAMS
TOTAL FIBRE	7	4	GRAMS
% CALORIES FROM FAT	17	17	

Scotch Oatmeal Bread

Sourdough is used for leavening in this tasty, nutritious bread. It has a wonderfully rich flavor. See page 44 for the recipe for sourdough starter batter.

1½-pound

½ cup sourdough starter batter

½ tablespoon cinnamon

1½ teaspoons salt

¼ teaspoon ginger

4 tablespoons dry milk

¾ tablespoon brown sugar

2½ cups bread flour

½ cup rolled oats

1½ tablespoons maple syrup

1½ tablespoons butter

1 cup warm water

1-pound

¼ cup + 2 tablespoons sourdough starter batter

1 teaspoon cinnamon

1 teaspoon salt

⅛ teaspoon ginger

2½ tablespoons dry milk

½ tablespoon brown sugar

1¾ cups bread flour

5 tablespoons rolled oats

1 tablespoon maple syrup

1 tablespoon butter

5½ ounces warm water

Instructions for baking:

Stop your machine at the end of the mix cycle. Reset the machine for delay. Program the machine to finish in 11 or 12 hours so that the mixed dough has time to react to the slow-acting sourdough leavening. If your machine has no delay feature, mix the dough, stop the machine, and let the dough rise for 8 hours before starting the machine again.

NUTRITIONAL ANALYSIS			
	1½-POUND	1-POUND	
TOTAL CALORIES	1994	1384	
TOTAL PROTEIN	64	44	GRAMS
TOTAL CARBOHYDRATES	369	258	GRAMS
TOTAL FAT	27	18	GRAMS
TOTAL SATURATED FAT	12	8	GRAMS
TOTAL CHOLESTEROL	51	34	MILLIGRAMS
TOTAL SODIUM	3351	2229	MILLIGRAMS
TOTAL FIBRE	11	7	GRAMS
% CALORIES FROM FAT	12	12	

Sourdough Potato Bread

This bread uses sourdough as the leavening instead of yeast. It has a firm texture with a good, sourdough flavor. See page 44 for the recipe for sourdough starter.

1½-pound	1-pound
½ cup sourdough starter batter	⅓ cup sourdough starter batter
½ teaspoon salt	¼ teaspoon salt
¼ teaspoon cream of tartar	⅛ teaspoon cream of tartar
¼ teaspoon baking soda	⅛ teaspoon baking soda
¼ cup dry milk	3 tablespoons dry milk
¼ cup instant mashed-potato flakes	3 tablespoons instant mashed-potato flakes
¼ teaspoon ginger	⅛ teaspoon ginger
2 tablespoons sugar	4 teaspoons sugar
2½ cups all-purpose flour	1¾ cups all-purpose flour
2½ tablespoons butter	2 tablespoons butter
7½ ounces warm water	5 ounces warm water

Note:

For DAK/Welbilt machines, use 2 additional tablespoons of warm water for the 1½-pound loaf.

Instructions for baking:

Stop your machine at the end of the mix cycle. Reset the machine for delay. Program the machine to finish in 11 or 12 hours, so that the mixed dough has time to react to the slow-acting sourdough leavening. If your machine has no delay feature, mix the dough, stop the machine, and let the dough rise for 8 hours before starting the machine again.

NUTRITIONAL ANALYSIS			
	1½-POUND	1-POUND	
TOTAL CALORIES	2000	1427	
TOTAL PROTEIN	60	42	GRAMS
TOTAL CARBOHYDRATES	348	243	GRAMS
TOTAL FAT	39	30	GRAMS

NUTRITIONAL ANALYSIS			
	1½-POUND	1-POUND	
TOTAL SATURATED FAT	19	15	GRAMS
TOTAL CHOLESTEROL	82	65	MILLIGRAMS
TOTAL SODIUM	1380	939	MILLIGRAMS
TOTAL FIBRE	6	4	GRAMS
% CALORIES FROM FAT	17	19	

APPENDIXES

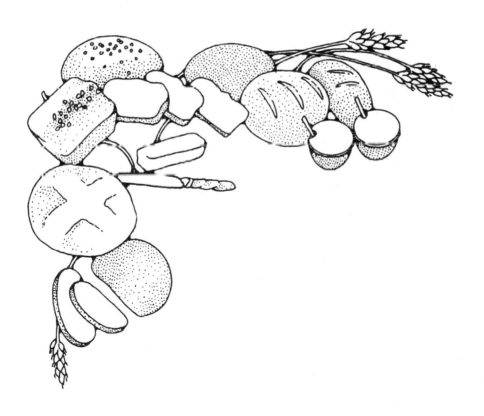

Measures

Dry Measure Equivalencies

To ➡ From	teaspoon	tablespoon	cup	pint
teaspoon	1	3	48	96
tablespoon	1/3	1	16	32
cup	1/48	1/16	1	2
pint	1/96	1/48	1/2	1

Liquid Measure Equivalencies

To ➡ From	teaspoon	tablespoon	ounce	cup	pint
teaspoon	1	3	6	48	96
tablespoon	1/3	1	2	16	32
ounce	1/6	1/2	1	8	16
cup	1/48	1/16	1/8	1	2
pint	1/96	1/48	1/16	1/2	1

Nutritional Quick Reference

All of the recipes in this book were analyzed for nutritional value. The following lists contain the top ten breads in each category, in order.

Highest-Fibre Breads

- Vollkornbrot
- Rieska Bread II
- Sunflower-Seed Whole-Wheat Bread
- Danish Sour Bread
- Viennese Hausbrot
- Hausbrot
- Finnish Rye Bread
- Soft Pumpernickel Bread
- Rieska Bread
- Portuguese Corn Bread

Lowest-Fat-Content Breads

- Diet Bread
- Cuban Bread
- Pane Italiano
- Adobe Bread II
- Forty-Niner Sourdough Bread
- Sour Rye Bread
- War Bread
- Viennese Hausbrot
- Hausbrot
- Vollkornbrot

Lowest-Calorie Breads

- Diet Bread
- Adobe Bread II
- Vollkornbrot
- Cuban Bread
- Pane Italiano
- Italian Whole-Wheat Bread
- Finnish Rye Bread
- Viennese Hausbrot
- English Oatmeal Bread
- Armenian Pita

Lowest-Sodium Breads

- Diet Bread
- Salt-Free White Bread
- Yorkshire Spice Bread
- Viennese Potato Bread
- Sunflower-Seed Whole-Wheat Bread
- Milk Bread
- Irish Barmbrack II
- Bohemian Houska Bread
- Finnish Easter-Crown Bread
- Viennese Striezel Bread

Overall Healthiest Breads

A formula was used to find the best 10 breads, based on their combination of low-calories, low-sodium, low-fat, and high-fibre content.

- Diet Bread
- Vollkornbrot
- Viennese Hausbrot
- Hausbrot
- Sunflower-Seed Whole-Wheat Bread
- War Bread
- Salt-Free White Bread
- Italian Whole-Wheat Bread
- Pane Italiano
- Danish Sour Bread

Bread Machine Information

Use the blanks to enter specific information about your bread machine and then use the chart for handy reference.

- ☐ Machine Brand _____
- ☐ Model Number _____
- ☐ Capacity (1 or 1½ pounds) _____
- ☐ Basic White-Bread Recipe:
    - ☐ ☐ Bread Flour _____
    - ☐ ☐ Ounces of Liquid _____
    - ☐ ☐ Liquidity Ratio _____

Index

About the Author

Norman A. Garrett, a college professor and expert in computers and technology, received his bachelor's degree from Brigham Young University, and his master's and doctoral degrees from Arizona State University. He enjoys cooking and baking, particularly outdoor cooking with old-fashioned Dutch ovens. He lives in rural Illinois with his wife, Margie, and their five children.